HERE IS THE ANSWER!
WHAT IS THE QUESTION?

Book 5 Covering
Robert's Rules of Order Newly Revised
11th edition
[Replaced books 1, 2, and 4]

© 2015
By American Institute of Parliamentarians
(888) 664-0428
www.aipparl.org
aip@aipparl.org

Produced in the United States of America.

ISBN 978-0-942736-39-7
Printed May 2015
1 2 3 4 5 6 7 8 9 10

Produced by the
Education Department
American Institute of Parliamentarians
Jeanette N. Williams, CP-T, Education Director
Ann Rempel, CPP-T, Printed Materials Division Chair
Alison Wallis, CP-T, President

INTRODUCTION

On the popular TV game show JEOPARDY!, the game board provides the answer and the contestants have to come up with the question. The game board contains five questions in each of six categories; and the three contestants compete against each other to be the first to "buzz in" to provide the question.

While the answers in this book all fall into one category, "Parliamentary Law" or "RONR," and the book doesn't have an electronic "buzz in" system, parliamentarians can now join in the fun and try their hand at finding the correct question to parliamentary answers.

Book 1 and Book 2 of this series provided over 1,600 answers (and questions) covering *Robert's Rules of Order Newly Revised,* 9th Edition. Book 4 covered *Robert's Rules of Order Newly Revised,* 10th Edition). This book replaces those books and provides 2,000 plus answers (and questions) covering *Robert's Rules of Order Newly Revised* **(RONR)** 11th Edition (2011). These answers (and questions) were prepared by the AIP Education Department. The answers and questions are grouped by the appropriate section in **RONR**. Each answer/question includes a reference to the page in **RONR** from which it was developed. Some are direct quotations, while others require applying the information from the referenced page.

ACKNOWLEDGEMENTS

The AIP Education Department is extremely grateful to Paul Lamb, CP-T, for writing this book and to Ruth Ryan, CP-T, and Carol Davis, CP-T, for their proofreading. In addition, the department is very appreciative of the work of Kay Allison Crews, CP, who formats publications for the AIP Education Department.

This page intentionally left blank.

SOME IDEAS ON HOW TO USE THIS BOOK

In the television game of JEOPARDY!, there is a host, three players, and an answer board consisting of six categories with five answers in each category. The answers are valued from $200 to $1,000 (double that in the double Jeopardy round,) which would indicate that they increase in difficulty as well. A player chooses a category and dollar amount, the host reads the answer, and the players compete to buzz in and provide the correct question. If their question is correct, the dollar amount is added to their total dollars; if their question is incorrect, the dollar amount of the answer is subtracted from their total (minus values are possible).

While this book can't provide you with buzzers and a big answer board, the book does contain lots of answers (along with the "correct" question). The answers and questions can be grouped for playing games like the television show.

Another way to use the answers is to transfer them to cards, shuffle the cards, and ask the answers in whatever order they are drawn from the shuffled deck.

Whatever way you choose, make it fun!

So, contestants, hands on your buzzers and get ready for a fast and fun session of:

Here is the Answer!

What is the Question?

This page intentionally left blank.

CONTENTS

This page intentionally left blank

CHAPTER I: THE DELIBERATIVE ASSEMBLY: ITS TYPES AND RULES

Section 1 - The Deliberative Assembly

Robert's Rules of Order Newly Revised, 11th Edition – Pages 1-10

1-1	A.	A type of gathering to which parliamentary law is generally understood to apply.	
	Q.	What is a deliberative assembly?	*RONR 1*
1-2	A.	An event to transact business.	
	Q.	What is a meeting?	*RONR 2*
1-3	A.	A person who is entitled to full participation in a meeting of an organization.	
	Q.	What is a member?	*RONR 3*
1-4	A.	More than half of the items (votes, members, etc.).	
	Q.	What is a majority?	*RONR 4*
1-5	A.	A notice of a proposal to be brought up at a meeting.	
	Q.	What is previous notice?	*RONR 4*
1-6	A.	The expressed approval of at least two-thirds of those present and voting.	
	Q.	What is a two-thirds vote?	*RONR 4*
1-7	A.	A written notice of a time and place for a meeting which is sent to all members of the organization.	
	Q.	What is the "call" of a meeting?	*RONR 4*
1-8	A.	The necessary minimum number of members who must be present to hold a meeting.	
	Q.	What is a quorum?	*RONR 5*
1-9	A.	A meeting of an unorganized group.	
	Q.	What is a mass meeting?	*RONR 5*
1-10	A.	A member whose rights are not under suspension	
	Q.	What is a member in good standing?	*RONR 6n*
1-11	A.	An assembly of delegates.	
	Q.	What is a convention?	*RONR 7*

Robert's Rules of Order Newly Revised, 11th Edition – Pages 10-19

2-1	A.	Corporate Charter, Constitution and/or Bylaws, Rules of Order, Special Rules of Order, and Standing Rules.
	Q.	What are various kinds of rules that may be formally adopted? ***RONR 10-11***

2-2	A.	Another name for Corporate Charter.
	Q.	What is a Certificate of Incorporation?
	Q.	What are Articles of Incorporation?
	Q.	What are Articles of Association? ***RONR 11***

2-3	A.	The document that should contain only what is necessary to obtain it and establish the desired status of the organization under law.
	Q.	What is a Corporate Charter? ***RONR 11-12***

2-4	A.	A document that defines the primary characteristics of the organization.
	Q.	What are bylaws? ***RONR 12***

2-5	A.	A document that prescribes how the organization functions.
	Q.	What are bylaws? ***RONR 13***

2-6	A.	The document which includes the rules that the organization considers so important that they cannot be changed without previous notice and a specified large vote.
	Q.	What are bylaws? ***RONR 13***

2-7	A.	A document that cannot be suspended (except for clauses which provide for their own suspension or clauses that are in the nature of a rule of order).
	Q.	What are bylaws? ***RONR 13***

2-8	A.	A document containing only the Name of the Organization, Object, Members, Officers, Meetings, and Amendment.
	Q.	What is a Constitution? ***RONR 13***

2-9	A.	A document containing the Name of the Organization, Object, Members, Officers, Meetings, Executive Board, Committees, Parliamentary Authority, and Amendment.
	Q.	What are bylaws? ***RONR 13***

2-10	A.	The document that supersedes the bylaws but yields to the corporate charter.
	Q.	What is the Constitution? ***RONR 14***

2-11	A.	The rules that relate to the orderly transaction of business meetings.
	Q.	What are rules of order? **RONR 15**

2-12	A.	An accepted manual of parliamentary law.
	Q.	What is a parliamentary authority? **RONR 15**

2-13	A.	The rules that supersede the rules contained in the parliamentary authority with which they may conflict.
	Q.	What are Special Rules of Order? **RONR 16**

2-14	A.	A rule adopted by a small assembly that its meetings will be governed by some or all of the somewhat less formal procedures applicable to small boards.
	Q.	What is a special rule of order? **RONR 16**

2-15	A.	Matters on which the organization's adopted parliamentary authority is silent.
	Q.	What is when provisions found in other works on parliamentary law can be persuasive but not binding on the body? **RONR 16-17**

2-16	A.	The vote necessary to suspend the rules contained in the parliamentary authority or special rules of order.
	Q.	What is a two-thirds vote? **RONR 17**

2-17	A.	The vote required for adoption or amendment of special rules of order contained within the bylaws.
	Q.	What is the procedure for amending the bylaws? **RONR 17**

2-18	A.	The rules containing the details of the administration of an organization.
	Q.	What are standing rules? **RONR 18**

2-19	A.	The vote required to adopt a new standing rule.
	Q.	What is a majority vote? **RONR 18**

2-20	A.	The vote required to suspend a standing rule.
	Q.	What is a majority vote? **RONR 18**

2-21	A.	The suspension of rule that has application outside a meeting context.
	Q.	What is a standing rule that cannot be suspended? **RONR 18**

2-22	A.	A particular practice that may sometimes come to be followed as if it were prescribed by a rule.
	Q.	What is a custom? **RONR 19**

CHAPTER II: THE CONDUCT OF BUSINESS
IN A DELIBERATIVE ASSEMBLY

Section 3 - Basic Provisions and Procedures

Robert's Rules of Order Newly Revised, 11th Edition - Pages 20-31

3-1	A.	The minimum number of members who must be present at a meeting for business to be validly transacted.
	Q.	What is a quorum? **RONR 21**
3-2	A.	The minimum essential officers for the conduct of business.
	Q.	What is a presiding officer and a secretary or clerk? **RONR 22**
3-3	A.	The presiding officer's official place or station.
	Q.	What is "the chair?" **RONR 22**
3-4	A.	The chair.
	Q.	What is another name for the presiding officer?
	Q.	What is the presiding officer's official place or station?
	Q.	What is how does the presiding officer refer to himself? **RONR 22**
3-5	A.	"Mr. President" or "Madam President" or his or her official title.
	Q.	What is how members address the presiding officer? **RONR 22-23**
3-6	A.	Mr. Chairman or Madam Chairman.
	Q.	What is how members address a person presiding at a meeting who has no regular title? **RONR 23**
3-7	A.	Your president or the chair.
	Q.	What is how the presiding officer refers to himself? **RONR 24**
3-8	A.	"The meeting will come to order" or "The meeting will be in order."
	Q.	What is what the presiding officer says when calling the meeting to order? **RONR 25**
3-9	A.	The sequence in which business is brought up or permitted to be introduced.
	Q.	What is an order of business? **RONR 25**
3-10	A.	The Reading and Approval of Minutes.
	Q.	What is the first item of business in an order of business? **RONR 26**
3-11	A.	The reports of Officers, Boards, and Standing Committees.
	Q.	What is the second item of business in an order of business?
	Q.	What is taken up immediately following the Reading and Approval of Minutes? **RONR 26**

3-12	A.	The reports of Special Committees.
	Q.	What is the third item of business in an order of business?
	Q.	What is taken up immediately following the Reports of Officers, Boards, and Standing Committees? ***RONR 26***

3-13	A.	Special Orders.
	Q.	What is the fourth item of business in an order of business?
	Q.	What is taken up immediately following Reports of Special Committees? ***RONR 26***

3-14	A.	Unfinished Business and General Orders.
	Q.	What is the fifth item of business in an order of business?
	Q.	What is taken up immediately following Special Orders? ***RONR 26***

3-15	A.	New Business.
	Q.	What is the sixth item of business in an order of business?
	Q.	What is taken up immediately following Unfinished Business and General Orders? ***RONR 26***

3-16	A.	The method by which business is brought before an assembly.
	Q.	What is a motion? ***RONR 27***

3-17	A.	A formal proposal made by a member in a meeting that the assembly take certain action.
	Q.	What is a motion? ***RONR 27***

3-18	A.	Rise and address the chair.
	Q.	What is how does a member obtain the floor? ***RONR 29***

3-19	A.	The chair recognizes a member.
	Q.	What is how does the chair give a member permission to speak? ***RONR 29***

3-20	A.	First right goes to the member who made the motion.
	Q.	What is the proper order in recognizing who is entitled to speak in debate? ***RONR 31***

Here is the Answer! What is the Question? Book 5

7

Section 4 –The Handling of a Motion

Robert's Rules of Order Newly Revised, 11th Edition - Pages 32-57

4-1	A.	A member makes a motion; another member seconds the motion; the chair states the question on the motion.
	Q.	What are the three steps for bringing a motion before the assembly? **RONR 32**

4-2	A.	After the chair has stated the motion.
	Q.	What is when is the motion pending? **RONR 32**

4-3	A.	The assembly adopts the motion.
	Q.	What is what the assembly does if it decides to do what the motion proposes? **RONR 32**

4-4	A.	The motion is lost or rejected.
	Q.	What is what happens to a motion if the assembly decides not to adopt it? **RONR 32**

4-5	A.	"I move that ..." or "I move the adoption of ..." or "I offer the following ... ."
	Q.	What are the words spoken by a member to introduce a motion? **RONR 33**

4-6	A.	Has the right to speak first in debate.
	Q.	What is the maker of the motion? **RONR 34, 42**

4-7	A.	"Is there a second to the motion?"
	Q.	What is what the chair asks to secure a second? **RONR 35**

4-8	A.	"The motion (or resolution) is not seconded." or "Since there is no second, the motion is not before this meeting."
	Q.	What is what the chair says when a motion has not received a second? **RONR 36**

4-9	A.	Another member agrees the motion should come before the meeting.
	Q.	What is a member seconds the motion? **RONR 36**

4-10	A.	When a motion is proposed by a committee or a board of more than one member.
	Q.	What is the motion does not require a second? **RONR 36**

4-11	A.	The time of the assembly is not consumed by having to dispose of a motion that only one person wants to see introduced.
	Q.	What is the purpose of a second? **RONR 36**

| 4-12 | A. | Before debate has begun, something a member can do if the chair states the question on a motion without waiting for a second. |
| | Q. | What is a member can raise a point of order? **RONR 37** |

| 4-13 | A. | Becomes immaterial once debate or voting has begun. |
| | Q. | What is a second to the motion? **RONR 37** |

| 4-14 | A. | The placing of a motion that has been made and seconded formally before the assembly. |
| | Q. | What is the meaning of the term "stating the question?" **RONR 37** |

| 4-15 | A. | "Is there any debate?" |
| | Q. | What is a less formal way of asking "Are you ready for the question?" **RONR 37-38** |

| 4-16 | A. | After the motion has been stated by the chair. |
| | Q. | What is when does a motion become the property of the assembly? **RONR 40** |

| 4-17 | A. | The maker of a motion can modify his motion or withdraw it entirely. |
| | Q. | What is what the maker of a motion can do before the chair states the motion? **RONR 40** |

| 4-18 | A. | Before it is stated by the chair, a member may request the maker to accept a modification to the motion. |
| | Q. | What is when may a member request the maker of a motion to accept a modification to the motion? **RONR 40** |

| 4-19 | A. | The member can withdraw his second if he doesn't agree with modifications to the motion prior to it being stated by the chair. |
| | Q. | What is what the member who seconds a motion can do if the maker of motion modifies it before the chair states the motion? **RONR 40** |

| 4-20 | A. | The chair says "The motion is withdrawn." |
| | Q. | What is the statement the chair makes when a motion has been withdrawn? **RONR 41** |

| 4-21 | A. | Members debate the motion, the chair puts the question, and the chair announces the results of the vote. |
| | Q. | What are the three steps for consideration of a motion? **RONR 42** |

| 4-22 | A. | Each member may speak twice on the same question on the same day. |
| | Q. | What is the number of times a member may speak in debate on a question? **RONR 43** |

| 4-23 | A. | After all members who have not spoken on a motion have had an opportunity to speak. |
| | Q. | What is when a member may make a second speech on a motion? **RONR 43** |

| 4-24 | A. | Ten minutes per speech. |
| | Q. | What is the length of time a member can make a speech in debate? **RONR 43** |

| 4-25 | A. | Debate must be confined to the merits of the pending motion. |
| | Q. | What is what a member can speak on in debate? **RONR 43** |

| 4-26 | A. | Situation when the presiding officer should not close debate. |
| | Q. | What is as long as any member who has not exhausted his right to debate desires the floor? **RONR 44** |

| 4-27 | A. | The phrase used by the chair when asking if any member wishes to debate the pending motion. |
| | Q. | What is "Are you ready for the question?" or "Is there any further debate?" **RONR 44** |

| 4-28 | A. | The chair calls for the vote on a motion. |
| | Q. | What is the meaning of the term "putting the question?" **RONR 44** |

| 4-29 | A. | The wording in the minutes should be the same as was stated by the chair. |
| | Q. | What is how is a motion recorded in the minutes? **RONR 44** |

| 4-30 | A. | Must always call for the negative vote. |
| | Q. | What is what the chair should do even when the affirmative vote appears unanimous? **RONR 45** |

| 4-31 | A. | A member does not vote. |
| | Q. | What is the meaning of "abstain?" **RONR 45** |

| 4-32 | A. | The regular method of voting on any motion that requires a majority vote for adoption. |
| | Q. | What is a voice vote? **RONR 45** |

| 4-33 | A. | "Those in favor of the motion, say *aye* ... Those opposed, say *no*." or "All those in favor ..." or "All in favor ... ." |
| | Q. | What is words the chair says to take a voice vote? **RONR 45** |

| 4-34 | A. | "Those in favor will rise (or stand) ... Be seated...Those opposed will rise (or stand) ... Be seated ...." |
| | Q. | What is what the chair says to take a rising (or standing) vote? **RONR 47** |

4-35	A.	"Those in favor will rise and remain standing until counted .... Be seated. Those opposed will rise and remain standing until counted .... Be seated."
	Q.	What is words the chair says to take a counted rising vote? **RONR 47**
4-36	A.	Up to the time when the results of a vote are announced.
	Q.	What is when may a member change his vote? **RONR 48**
4-37	A.	"Division!" or "I call for a division" or "I doubt the result of the vote."
	Q.	What is what a member says to require a voice vote to be retaken by a rising vote? **RONR 52**
4-38	A.	The chair votes only when his vote would affect the outcome.
	Q.	What is how the chair maintains his impartial position? **RONR 53**
4-39	A.	Unanimous (or General) Consent.
	Q.	What is the method of approval that may be used when there seems to be little or no opposition? **RONR 54**
4-40	A.	"If there is no objection ..." or "Without objection ..." or "Is there any objection to ...?"
	Q.	What is what the chair says to obtain unanimous consent? **RONR 54**
4-41	A.	The correction and approval of minutes is an example.
	Q.	What is business normally handled by unanimous consent? **RONR 55**

CHAPTER III: DESCRIPTION OF MOTIONS
IN ALL CLASSIFICATIONS

Section 5 - Basic Classification; Order of Precedence of Motions

Robert's Rules of Order Newly Revised, 11th Edition - Pages 58-62

5-1	A.	Term applied to subsidiary, incidental, and privileged motions.
	Q.	What are secondary motions? **RONR 58-59**
5-2	A.	Number of major classes of motions.
	Q.	What is five? **RONR 59**
5-3	A.	These two classes of motions are not secondary motions.
	Q.	What are main motions and motions that bring the question again before the assembly? **RONR 59**
5-4	A.	The number of motions under direct consideration at any time.
	Q.	What is one? **RONR 59**
5-5	A.	Certain matters that can be introduced without disposing of the pending question.
	Q.	What are privileged questions? **RONR 59**
5-6	A.	The question currently being considered by the assembly.
	Q.	What is the immediately pending question? **RONR 60**
5-7	A.	"The question is on the motion to ...."
	Q.	What is how the chair informs the assembly of the pending question? **RONR 60**
5-8	A.	The term used to indicate priority of one motion over another.
	Q.	What is precedence? **RONR 60**
5-9	A.	The term used when a motion ranks higher than another motion to become the immediately pending question.
	Q.	What is takes precedence over? **RONR 60**

Section 6 - Description of Classes and Individual Motions

Robert's Rules of Order Newly Revised, 11th Edition - Pages 62-79

6-1	A.	The lowest ranking motion.	
	Q.	What is a main motion?	***RONR 62***
6-2	A.	The class of motions which helps dispose of a main motion.	
	Q.	What are Subsidiary Motions?	***RONR 62***
6-3	A.	The motion that will enable the assembly to avoid a direct vote on an embarrassing main motion.	
	Q.	What is Postpone Indefinitely?	***RONR 63***
6-4	A.	The subsidiary motion that can modify the main motion.	
	Q.	What is Amend?	***RONR 63***
6-5	A.	The motion that proposes to have the main motion considered by a smaller group, a committee.	
	Q.	What is Commit or Refer?	***RONR 63***
6-6	A.	The motion that will allow the consideration of the main motion at a different and specific time.	
	Q.	What is Postpone to a Certain Time (or Postpone Definitely)?	***RONR 64***
6-7	A.	The motion that will change the length of speeches made during debate.	
	Q.	What is Limit or Extend Limits of Debate?	***RONR 64***
6-8	A.	The motion that will close debate and cause an immediate vote.	
	Q.	What is Previous Question?	***RONR 64***
6-9	A.	The motion that will set aside the main motion temporarily.	
	Q.	What is Lay on the Table?	***RONR 64***
6-10	A.	They are out of order when another member has the floor.	
	Q.	What is a distinguishing characteristic of subsidiary motions as a class?	***RONR 64-65***
6-11	A.	Incidental main motions corresponding to subsidiary motions that can be made when no other motion is pending.	
	Q.	What are the first five subsidiary motions; Postpone Indefinitely, Amend, Commit or Refer; Postpone to a Certain Time (or Definitely) and Limit or Extend Limits of Debate?	***RONR 66***
6-12	A.	The class of motions of overriding importance to the assembly.	
	Q.	What are privileged motions?	***RONR 66***

| 6-13 | A. | The motion that will bring the assembly back to its scheduled business. | |
| | Q. | What is Call for the Orders of the Day? | **RONR 67** |

| 6-14 | A. | The motion that permits the interruption of pending business to make an urgent request affecting a right or privilege of the assembly or of an individual member. | |
| | Q. | What is Raise a Question of Privilege? | **RONR 67** |

| 6-15 | A. | The motion, if adopted, that will allow for a short intermission in a meeting even while business is pending. | |
| | Q. | What is Recess? | **RONR 67** |

| 6-16 | A. | The motion, if adopted, that will end the meeting. | |
| | Q. | What is Adjourn? | **RONR 68** |

| 6-17 | A. | The motion that will establish a continuation of this meeting. | |
| | Q. | What is Fix the Time to Which to Adjourn? | **RONR 68** |

| 6-18 | A. | Incidental Main Motions corresponding to Privileged Motions that can be made when no other motion is pending. | |
| | Q. | What are the motions Recess, to Adjourn, and to Fix the Time to Which to Adjourn? | **RONR 68** |

| 6-19 | A. | A class of motions which do not have rank among themselves but are related to the business otherwise at hand. | |
| | Q. | What are incidental motions? | **RONR 69** |

| 6-20 | A. | The class of motions which relate to questions of procedure arising out of the business of the assembly, past or present, or another motion or item of business. | |
| | Q. | What are incidental motions? | **RONR 69** |

| 6-21 | A. | The motion that will call attention to the violation of a rule. | |
| | Q. | What is Point of Order? | **RONR 70** |

| 6-22 | A. | The motion made when a member believes the chair made an improper ruling. | |
| | Q. | What is Appeal? | **RONR 70** |

| 6-23 | A. | The motion that will allow the assembly to do something that is in violation of one of its regular rules. | |
| | Q. | What is Suspend the Rules? | **RONR 70** |

| 6-24 | A. | The motion that will avoid any discussion or vote on the main motion. | |
| | Q. | What is Objection to the Consideration of the Question? | **RONR 70** |

6-25	A.	The motion that will separate a main motion into two or more parts.	
	Q.	What is Division of a Question?	**RONR 70-71**

6-26	A.	The motion that permits the consideration of a lengthy main motion containing several paragraphs or sections by parts.	
	Q.	What is Consider by Paragraph or Seriatim?	**RONR 71**

6-27	A.	The motion that demands a voice vote be retaken as a standing vote.	
	Q.	What is Division of the Assembly?	**RONR 71**

6-28	A.	The motions which determine how a vote of the members will be taken, or the opening and closing of the polls.	
	Q.	What are Motions Relating to Methods of Voting and the Polls?	**RONR 71**

6-29	A.	The motions which determine how the assembly will select possible candidates for election to office.	
	Q.	What are Motions Relating to Nominations?	**RONR 71**

6-30	A.	The motion a member can make when a member wishes to be relieved from an obligation.	
	Q.	What is Request to Be Excused from a Duty?	**RONR 71-72**

6-31	A.	When the chair is asked a question concerning a parliamentary process.	
	Q.	What is Parliamentary Inquiry?	**RONR 72**

6-32	A.	When the chair is asked a question about facts affecting the business at hand.	
	Q.	What is Request for Information?	**RONR 72**

6-33	A.	When a member decides that the motion he made, after it has been stated by the chair, should not be considered.	
	Q.	What is Request for Permission (or Leave) to Withdraw or Modify a Motion?	**RONR 72**

6-34	A.	When a member wishes to quote or read an article, or a book, as a part of his speech.	
	Q.	What is Request to Read Papers?	**RONR 72**

6-35	A.	The class of motions which returns to the assembly motions temporarily disposed of or previously adopted.	
	Q.	What are the "bring again" motions?	
	Q.	What are Motions that Bring a Question Again Before the Assembly?	**RONR 74-75**

6-36	A.	While a question is temporarily disposed of but is not finally settled, no similar or conflicting motion whose adoption would restrict the assembly in acting on the first question can be introduced.
	Q.	What is a principals of parliamentary law that may be seen as related to Motions that Bring a Question Again Before the Assembly? **RONR 75**
6-37	A.	The motion that will allow the assembly to resume consideration of a main motion temporarily set aside.
	Q.	What is Take from the Table? **RONR 75-76**
6-38	A.	The motion that would negate or amend action taken last year.
	Q.	What is Rescind or Amend Something Previously Adopted? **RONR 76**
6-39	A.	The motion that would return a question or an assigned task from a small group to the full assembly.
	Q.	What is Discharge a Committee? **RONR 76**
6-40	A.	The motion at the same meeting (or the next day in the same session on which a business meeting is held) that will return for further consideration a motion that has been adopted or defeated.
	Q.	What is Reconsider? **RONR 76**

Robert's Rules of Order Newly Revised, 11th Edition - Pages 79-80

| 7-1 | A. | The important rules governing the use of individual motions. | |
| | Q. | What are the standard descriptive characteristics? | **RONR 79** |

| 7-2 | A. | Whether it is in order or not when another has the floor. | |
| | Q. | What is can the motion interrupt or not interrupt a speaker? | ***RONR 80*** |

| 7-3 | A. | Needed for most motions to indicate the assembly's interest. | |
| | Q. | What is a second? | ***RONR 80*** |

| 7-4 | A. | A main motion requires this, unless it is made by the direction of a board or committee (of more than one member). | |
| | Q. | What is a second? | ***RONR 80*** |

| 7-5 | A. | The motion can be discussed by the assembly. | |
| | Q. | What is debatable? | ***RONR 80*** |

| 7-6 | A. | The motion can be modified. | |
| | Q. | What is amendable? | ***RONR 80*** |

| 7-7 | A. | The motion can be approved by a majority, two thirds, or another number of votes cast. | |
| | Q. | What is the vote required for adoption of a motion? | ***RONR 80*** |

| 7-8 | A. | The motion may be brought back for further consideration. | |
| | Q. | What is whether the motion can be reconsidered? | ***RONR 80*** |

CHAPTER IV: MEETING AND SESSION

Section 8 - Meeting, Session, Recess, Adjournment

Robert's Rules of Order Newly Revised, 11th Edition - Pages 81-88

8-1	A.	A single official gathering of members in one room to transact business for a length of time during which there is no cessation of proceedings and the members do not separate, unless for a short recess.
	Q.	What is a meeting? **RONR 81-82**
8-2	A.	A meeting or a series of connected meetings devoted to a single order of business, program, agenda, or announced purpose.
	Q.	What is a session? **RONR 82**
8-3	A.	A short intermission within a meeting that does not end the meeting or destroy its continuity as a single gathering.
	Q.	What is a recess? **RONR 82**
8-4	A.	A brief pause in a meeting without the declaration of a recess.
	Q.	What is stand at ease? **RONR 82**
8-5	A.	The act of terminating a meeting or ending a session.
	Q.	What is adjournment? **RONR 82-83**
8-6	A.	A long break that does terminate a meeting but not the session.
	Q.	What is adjournment? **RONR 82-83**
8-7	A.	The close of a session of several meetings where the assembly is dissolved and the body will not meet again until the time prescribed by the bylaws or constitution unless called into special session.
	Q.	What is adjournment sine die? **RONR 83**
8-8	A.	Term for the meetings of an organization that are held regularly and complete an established order of business in a single afternoon or evening.
	Q.	What is a session? **RONR 83**
8-9	A.	A convention of an organization having one agenda which may be broken up into separate meetings over several days.
	Q.	What is a session? **RONR 84**
8-10	A.	At the conclusion of a recess business is resumed where it was left off and there are no opening ceremonies.
	Q.	What is the difference between an "adjournment" and a "recess?" **RONR 85**

8-11	A.	A way that the time or provision for the next meeting or a session may have been established.
	Q.	What is a program adopted at the beginning of a convention?
	Q.	What is the adoption of a motion to Fix the Time to Which to Adjourn?
	Q.	What is a specification in the motion to Adjourn? ***RONR 85-86***
8-12	A.	The ordinary practice of closing a meeting.
	Q.	What is adopting the motion Adjourn? ***RONR 86***
8-13	A.	The chair should declare the meeting adjourned to a time and place for an adjourned meeting or to meet at the call of the chair.
	Q.	What is what the chair should do in the event of an extreme emergency? ***RONR 86***
8-14	A.	The principal significance of a session.
	Q.	What is the freedom of each new session? ***RONR 86-87***
8-15	A.	One session cannot tie the hands of the majority at a later one.
	Q.	What is the freedom of each new session? ***RONR 87***
8-16	A.	Rules that do not deal with parliamentary procedure.
	Q.	What are standing rules? ***RONR 87***
8-17	A.	A rule that can be suspended for the duration of a session by a majority vote.
	Q.	What is a standing rule? ***RONR 87***
8-18	A.	Rules that require both previous notice and a two-thirds vote for amendment.
	Q.	What are bylaws and special rules of order which deal with parliamentary procedure? ***RONR 87-88***
8-19	A.	Rules that require a two-thirds vote for suspension.
	Q.	What are rules of order? ***RONR 88***
8-20	A.	A motion that was made at a previous session and was lost, but is introduced at the present session as if it were new.
	Q.	What is "renewed"? ***RONR 88***
8-21	A.	Required for choosing a chairman pro tem to serve beyond the present session.
	Q.	What is previous notice and election? ***RONR 88***

Section 9 - Particular Types of Business Meetings

Robert's Rules of Order Newly Revised, 11th Edition - Pages 89-99

9-1	A.	A periodic business meeting of a permanent society held weekly, monthly, quarterly or at similar intervals for which the day should be prescribed by the bylaws.
	Q.	What is a regular meeting? **RONR 89**
9-2	A.	Sent by postal mail to the member's last known address or sent by a form of electronic communication such as e-mail or fax by which the member has agreed to receive notice.
	Q.	What is written notice sent to each member? **RONR 89**
9-3	A.	The second session begins at any time during or before the third calendar month after the calendar month in which the first session ends.
	Q.	What is holding the meetings within a quarterly time interval? **RONR 89-90**
9-4	A.	The means by which a motion can go over to another session when the session is held beyond a quarterly time interval.
	Q.	What is referral to a committee? **RONR 91**
9-5	A.	A session that is held to deal with important matters that require action between regular meetings.
	Q.	What is a special meeting? **RONR 91**
9-6	A.	A separate session of a society held at a time different from that of any regular meeting and convened only to consider one or more items of business specified in the call of the meeting.
	Q.	What is a special meeting? **RONR 91**
9-7	A.	A notice of the time, place, and exact purpose of the meeting clearly and specifically describing the subject matter of the motions or items of business to be brought up must be sent to all members.
	Q.	What is in the call of a special meeting? **RONR 91**
9-8	A.	By whom a special meeting can be called and the number of days' notice required.
	Q.	What is bylaws provisions concerning special meetings? **RONR 92**
9-9	A.	A meeting which is a continuation of the business of the immediately preceding regular or special meeting.
	Q.	What is an adjourned meeting? **RONR 93**
9-10	A.	A stated meeting.
	Q.	What is a regular meeting? **RONR 94**

9-11	A.	A called meeting.	
	Q.	What is a special meeting?	**RONR 94**

9-12	A.	The first item of business of an adjourned meeting.	
	Q.	What is the reading of the minutes of the preceding meeting?	**RONR 94**

9-13	A.	A meeting held once a year.	
	Q.	What is an annual meeting?	**RONR 94**

9-14	A.	A meeting where the reports of officers and standing committees are given and officers are elected.	
	Q.	What is an annual meeting?	**RONR 94**

9-15	A.	The annual meeting minutes are read at the next regular meeting.	
	Q.	What is when the annual meeting minutes are read in an organization that meets quarterly or more often?	**RONR 95**

9-16	A.	A meeting or a portion of a meeting held in secret.	
	Q.	What is an executive session?	**RONR 95**

9-17	A.	Type of motion used to go into executive session.	
	Q.	What is a question of privilege?	**RONR 95**

9-18	A.	The record of proceedings of an executive session are read and acted on in executive session unless the action taken was not secret or secrecy has been lifted by the assembly.	
	Q.	What is how minutes of an executive session are acted upon?	**RONR 96**

9-19	A.	The brief minutes of an executive session held solely for the purpose of approving the minutes of a previous executive session.	
	Q.	What is are assumed to be approved by that meeting?	**RONR 96**

9-20	A.	A meeting where members communicate with other members through the Internet or by telephone.	
	Q.	What is an electronic meeting?	**RONR 97**

9-21	A.	A meeting authorized by the bylaws that is treated as though it were a meeting at which all members participating are actually present.	
	Q.	What is an electronic meeting?	**RONR 97**

9-22	A.	An essential characteristic of an electronic meeting.	
	Q.	What is simultaneous aural communication?	**RONR 98**

9-23	A.	The document that can authorized established committees to hold valid electronic meetings,	
	Q.	What are the bylaws?	**RONR 98**

CHAPTER V: THE MAIN MOTION

Section 10 – The Main Motion

Robert's Rules of Order Newly Revised, 11th Edition - Pages 100-25

10-1	A.	The motion which brings business before the assembly.
	Q.	What is a Main Motion? **RONR 100**
10-2	A.	The two types of main motions.
	Q.	What is an Original Main Motion and an Incidental Main Motion? **RONR 100**
10-3	A.	The motion that introduces a substantive question as a new subject.
	Q.	What is an Original Main Motion? **RONR 100**
10-4	A.	A motion presented when there is no business before the assembly that relates to business of the assembly or its past or future action.
	Q.	What is an Incidental Main Motion? **RONR 101**
10-5	A.	The main motion which does not mark the beginning of a particular involvement of the assembly in a substantive matter.
	Q.	What is an Incidental Main Motion? **RONR 101**
10-6	A.	One purpose of this type of main motion is to adopt the recommendations of a committee.
	Q.	What is an Incidental Main Motion? **RONR 101**
10-7	A.	One purpose of this type of main motion is to ratify emergency action taken at a meeting without a quorum.
	Q.	What is an Incidental Main Motion? **RONR 101**
10-8	A.	The motion *Objection to the Consideration of a Question* can be applied only to an original main motion.
	Q.	What is the chief difference in rules governing Original and Incidental Main Motions? **RONR 102**
10-9	A.	The motions over which the main motion takes precedence.
	Q.	What is none? **RONR 102**
10-10	A.	Should be worded in a concise, unambiguous, and complete form appropriate to such a purpose.
	Q.	What is the wording of a main motion? **RONR 104**
10-11	A.	A main motion that directs the assembly to affirm a previous position of the assembly.
	Q.	What is not in order? **RONR 104**

10-12	A.	A main motion that directs the assembly to refrain from doing something.
	Q.	What is a motion that should not be made? **RONR 104**
10-13	A.	A lengthy main motion that may contain several paragraphs.
	Q.	What is a Resolution? **RONR 105**
10-14	A.	The number of resolving clauses permitted in a resolution.
	Q.	What is one or more? **RONR 106**
10-15	A.	The reasons for adopting the motion included in a "resolution."
	Q.	What is a preamble of a "resolution"? **RONR 106-07**
10-16	A.	Provides a brief statement of background in a resolution.
	Q.	What is the preamble? **RONR 107**
10-17	A.	The word which precedes each preamble paragraph.
	Q.	What is "Whereas"? **RONR 107**
10-18	A.	The requirement for a preamble in a resolution.
	Q.	What is not required? **RONR 107**
10-19	A.	The rule concerning periods in a preamble to a resolution.
	Q.	What is should not contain any? **RONR 108**
10-20	A.	The rule concerning the word following "Whereas" and *Resolved* in a resolution.
	Q.	What is first letter is capitalized? **RONR 108**
10-21	A.	The word used in place of *Resolved* in instructions to an employee.
	Q.	What is *Ordered*? **RONR 110**
10-22	A.	The number of related resolutions which can be offered at one time.
	Q.	What is one or more? **RONR 110**
10-23	A.	A motion which conflicts with the bylaws or other rules of the organization or assembly or procedural rules prescribed by national, state, or local law.
	Q.	What is not in order? **RONR 111**
10-24	A.	A main motion which presents substantially the same question as a motion that was finally disposed of earlier in the same session by being rejected, postponed indefinitely or subjected to an Objection to the Consideration of a Question that was sustained.
	Q.	What is not in order? **RONR 111**

10-25	A.	A main motion rejected at an earlier session
	Q.	What is can be introduced again as if new at any later session? **RONR 111**

10-26	A.	A main motion rejected earlier in a session may become pending.
	Q.	What is adoption of a motion to reconsider the vote? **RONR 111**

10-27	A.	A main motion that conflicts with a motion previously adopted at any time and still in force.
	Q.	What is not in order? **RONR 111**

10-28	A.	A motion that would conflict with or presents substantially the same question as one which has been temporarily but not finally disposed of and remains within the control of the assembly.
	Q.	What is not in order? **RONR 112**

10-29	A.	A motion that proposes action outside the scope of the organization's object as defined in the bylaws or corporate charter.
	Q.	What is not in order unless by a two-thirds vote the assembly authorizes its introduction? **RONR 113**

10-30	A.	The usual method used to improve or modify a Main Motion.
	Q.	What is Amend? **RONR 115**

10-31	A.	The number of motions which can be pending at any one time.
	Q.	What is the main motion and one or more subsidiary or incidental motions? **RONR 116**

10-32	A.	The two motions which allow the introduction of a new main motion while a main motion is under consideration.
	Q.	What is Call for the Orders of the Day and Raise a Question of Privilege? **RONR 118**

10-33	A.	The title for the chair when no title is prescribed by the bylaws.
	Q.	What is Chairman? (Mr. or Madam.) **RONR 119**

10-34	A.	A term describing a necessary condition for the adoption of certain motions.
	Q.	What is previous notice? **RONR 121**

10-35	A.	The requirement to adopt a motion to Rescind, Amend Something Previously Adopted, or to Discharge a Committee by majority vote.
	Q.	What is previous notice? **RONR 122**

10-36	A.	The usual required announcement at the previous meeting in order to consider an amendment to the bylaws.
	Q.	What is previous notice? **RONR 122**

10-37 A.	Meaning to accept or to agree to.	
Q.	What is the term "Adopt"?	**RONR 124**
10-38 A.	To accept a report or recommendations of a standing committee prepared on the committee's own initiative.	
Q.	What is "Adopt"?	**RONR 124**
10-39 A.	The motion to confirm action already taken that cannot become legally valid until approved in the assembly.	
Q.	What is "Ratify"?	**RONR 124**
10-40 A.	The motion to approve or confirm action improperly taken at a meeting at which no quorum was present.	
Q.	What is "Ratify"?	**RONR 124**
10-41 A.	The motion to approve action taken by officers, committees, delegates, or subordinate bodies in excess of their instructions or authority.	
Q.	What is "Ratify"?	**RONR 124**
10-42 A.	The motion to approve action taken by a local unit which requires concurrence by the state or national organization or action taken by a state or national organization subject to approval by its constituent units.	
Q.	What is "Ratify"?	**RONR 125**

CHAPTER VI: SUBSIDIARY MOTIONS

Section 11 – Postpone Indefinitely

Robert's Rules of Order Newly Revised, 11th Edition - Pages 126-30

11-1	A.	The subsidiary motion that allows the assembly to decline taking a position on a main question.	
	Q.	What is Postpone Indefinitely?	**RONR 126**
11-2	A.	The subsidiary motion can kill a main motion.	
	Q.	What is Postpone Indefinitely?	**RONR 126**
11-3	A.	The motion that take precedence over only the main motion.	
	Q.	What is to Postpone Indefinitely?	**RONR 126**
11-4	A.	The subsidiary motion, if adopted, that suppresses the main motion for the remainder of the session.	
	Q.	What is to Postpone Indefinitely?	**RONR 127-28**
11-5	A.	The motion that is dropped when a main motion is referred to a committee.	
	Q.	What is to Postpone Indefinitely?	**RONR 128**
11-6	A.	The motion that is used to test the strength of the opponents to a main motion.	
	Q.	What is to Postpone Indefinitely?	**RONR 128**
11-7	A.	The motion that gives members who have exhausted their times to speak another chance to debate the main motion.	
	Q.	What is to Postpone Indefinitely?	**RONR 128**
11-8	A.	A motion which gives the opponents two chances to debate and defeat the main motion.	
	Q.	What is to Postpone Indefinitely?	**RONR 128**

Section 12 - Amend

Robert's Rules of Order Newly Revised, 11th Edition - Pages 130-67

12-1	A.	A motion which modifies the wording of another motion.	
	Q.	What is Amend?	***RONR 130***
12-2	A.	It is probably the most widely used subsidiary motion.	
	Q.	What is Amend?	***RONR 130***
12-3	A.	The only group that can make an amendment to a motion.	
	Q.	What is the assembly?	***RONR 131***
12-4	A.	This term means closely related to or having bearing on the subject.	
	Q.	What is germane?	***RONR 131***
12-5	A.	This motion when applied to motions other than main motions, can take precedence over motions of higher rank.	
	Q.	What is Amend?	***RONR 131***
12-6	A.	The only motion which can be applied to itself.	
	Q.	What is Amend?	***RONR 132***
12-7	A.	A subsidiary motion that can have the motion Division of the Question or Consideration by Paragraph or Seriatim applied to it.	
	Q.	What is Amend?	***RONR 132***
12-8	A.	This subsidiary motion is not always debatable.	
	Q.	What is Amend?	***RONR 133***
12-9	A.	The preferred name of an amendment to an amendment.	
	Q.	What is secondary amendment?	***RONR 133***
12-10	A.	The three processes of amending.	
	Q.	What is "insert or add," "strike out," and "strike out and insert"?	***RONR 134-35***
12-11	A.	A motion which inserts words in or adds words at the end of another motion.	
	Q.	What is to amend by "inserting" or "adding"?	***RONR 134***
12-12	A.	A motion which removes words from another motion.	
	Q.	What is to amend by "striking out"?	***RONR 134***
12-13	A.	The name for the amendment process to "strike out and insert" when applied to paragraphs.	
	Q.	What is to substitute?	***RONR 134***

12-14	A.	An amendment of the third degree.
	Q.	What is not permitted? **RONR 135**
12-15	A.	The total number of amendments which can be pending at a time.
	Q.	What is one primary and one secondary amendment? **RONR 135**
12-16	A.	The number of primary amendments which can be applied to a main motion.
	Q.	What is unlimited (but only one at a time)? **RONR 135**
12-17	A.	An amendment must in some way involve the same subject that is raised by the motion to which it is applied.
	Q.	What is meant by "to be germane"? **RONR 136**
12-18	A.	When the essential idea of an amendment cannot be introduced in-dependently at the same session.
	Q.	What is the amendment is germane and should be admitted? **RONR 136**
12-19	A.	An amendment that makes the adoption of the amended motion the same as rejection of the unamended motion.
	Q.	What is an improper amendment? **RONR 138**
12-20	A.	An amendment that would cause the motion as amended to become out of order.
	Q.	What is an improper amendment? **RONR 138**
12-21	A.	An amendment that changes the form of amendment into another form of amendment.
	Q.	What is an improper amendment? **RONR 138**
12-22	A.	An amendment that changes one parliamentary motion into a differ-ent parliamentary motion.
	Q.	What is an improper amendment? · **RONR 138-39**
12-23	A.	An amendment that strikes out the word "*Resolved*" or other enact-ing words.
	Q.	What is an improper amendment? **RONR 139**
12-24	A.	The part of a resolution that is amended last.
	Q.	What is the preamble? **RONR 139**
12-25	A.	Identifies where words inserted by an amendment are placed.
	Q.	What is the word before, the word after, or the words between which? **RONR 139-40**

12-26 A.	Where the words added by an amendment are placed.	
Q.	What is amend by adding at the end?	**RONR 140**

12-27 A.	The time when words proposed to be inserted or added can be perfected.	
Q.	What is before adoption of the primary amendment?	**RONR 140**

12-28 A.	The forms of secondary amendments which can be applied to a primary amendment to "insert or to add words."	
Q.	What is "insert or add," "strike out," and "strike out and insert?"	**RONR 141**

12-29 A.	State the question as for any other motion.	
Q.	What is the first step for stating the question on an amendment?	**RONR 142**

12-30 A.	Read the main motion or the affected portion as it would stand if the amendment was adopted.	
Q.	What is the second step for stating the motion on an amendment?	**RONR 142**

12-31 A.	Make it clear once more that it is the amendment that is under immediate consideration.	
Q.	What is the third step for stating the motion on an amendment?	**RONR 142**

12-32 A.	Repeat the amendment.	
Q.	What is the first step for putting to a vote a motion on an amendment?	**RONR 142**

12-33 A.	Take the vote in such a way as to make clear it is the amendment that is to be voted on.	
Q.	What is the third step for putting to a vote a motion on an amendment?	**RONR 143**

12-34 A.	Happens when an amendment is so simple or acceptable.	
Q.	What is adoption by unanimous consent?	**RONR 145**

12-35 A.	A form of the motion *Amend* that can only be applied to consecutive words.	
Q.	What is an amendment by "striking out" words?	**RONR 146**

12-36 A.	The form of secondary amendment which can be applied to a primary amendment to "strike out" words.	
Q.	What is only to "strike out?"	**RONR 146**

Here is the Answer! What is the Question? Book 5

29

12-37	A.	After the adoption of the primary amendment the words will remain in the main motion.
	Q.	What is the result of "striking out" words in a primary amendment? **RONR 146**

12-38	A.	The form of amendment which allows the words to be struck out to be amended prior to voting on the amendment.
	Q.	What is to "strike out" a paragraph? (Also see "substitute") **RONR 147**

12-39	A.	The forms of secondary amendments which can be applied to the paragraph to be struck out.
	Q.	What is "to insert or add words," "strike out words," and "strike out and insert words?" **RONR 147**

12-40	A.	Words struck out of a primary amendment to strike out a paragraph when primary amendment is not adopted.
	Q.	What is words are struck out of main motion? **RONR 148**

12-41	A.	The motion to replace words with different words.
	Q.	What is to amend by "striking out and inserting"? **RONR 149**

12-42	A.	The motion which removes words from one place and put the same words in another place.
	Q.	What is to amend by "striking out and inserting"? **RONR 149**

12-43	A.	The forms of secondary amendments which can be applied to a primary amendment to "strike out and insert."
	Q.	What is "insert or add," "strike out," and "strike out and insert"? **RONR 150**

12-44	A.	Secondary amendments to the words to be struck out are taken up first and then secondary amendments to the words to be inserted are considered.
	Q.	What is the sequence for secondary amendments to the motion to amend by striking out and inserting? **RONR 150**

12-45	A.	An entire paragraph, section or article, or a complete main motion or resolution is struck out and a different paragraph, section or article, or motion or resolution is inserted in its place.
	Q.	What is amendment by substitution? **RONR 153**

12-46	A.	The forms of secondary amendments which can be applied to a primary amendment to substitute.
	Q.	What is "insert or add," "strike out," and "strike out and insert or substitute?" **RONR 154**

12-47 A.	The part usually considered first in handling the motion to substitute.	
Q.	What is debate and amend the paragraph to be struck out?	
		RONR 154

12-48 A.	This motion allows more than three choices to be considered.	
Q.	What is to create a blank?	**RONR 162**

12-49 A.	The number of choices which can be offered for consideration to fill a blank.	
Q.	What is unlimited?	**RONR 162**

12-50 A.	The usual items for filling a blank.	
Q.	What are names of persons or places, dates, numbers, or amounts?	
		RONR 164

12-51 A.	The number of suggestions for filling a blank (except when the blank can be filled with more than one name) that can be made by a single member.	
Q.	What is one without unanimous consent?	**RONR 164**

12-52 A.	The order on which names are voted on for filling a blank.	
Q.	What is same order as proposed?	**RONR 164**

12-53 A.	This ends the voting process for filling a single blank.	
Q.	What is when a suggestion receives a majority vote?	**RONR 164**

12-54 A.	The order on which amounts of money are voted on for filling a blank to purchase something.	
Q.	What is highest to lowest?	**RONR 165**

12-55 A.	The order on which amounts of money are voted on for filling a blank to sell something.	
Q.	What is smallest to largest?	**RONR 166**

12-56 A.	The general rule for the order of voting when filling a blank with places.	
Q.	What is same order as proposed?	**RONR 166**

12-57 A.	The general rule for the order of voting when filling a blank with a proposal.	
Q.	What is start with the one least likely to be accepted?	**RONR 166**

12-58 A.	The general rule for the order when there is no clear-cut reason to do otherwise in filling a blank with places, dates, or numbers.	
Q.	What is largest number, longest time, or most distant date, etc.?	
		RONR 166

Section 13 – Commit or Refer

Robert's Rules of Order Newly Revised, 11th Edition - Pages 168-79

13-1	A.	The motion that sends a main motion (and pending amendments, if any) to a smaller group of selected persons.
	Q.	What is Commit or Refer? **RONR 168**
13-2	A.	The three variations of the motion to commit or refer.
	Q.	What is to "go into a committee of the whole," to "go into quasi committee of the whole," or to "consider informally"? **RONR 168**
13-3	A.	The simplest variation of the motion to Commit or Refer involving the whole assembly.
	Q.	What is informal consideration? **RONR 168**
13-4	A.	The term used when sending a motion back to a committee.
	Q.	What is to recommit? **RONR 168**
13-5	A.	A dilatory motion to commit.
	Q.	What is what the chair should rule out of order? **RONR 172**
13-6	A.	Members can offer suggestions or formal amendments to complete the required details.
	Q.	What is when a motion to Commit lacks essential details? **RONR 172**
13-7	A.	Committee of the whole; quasi committee of the whole; consider informally; standing committees (in the order in which they are proposed); and special committees.
	Q.	What are the different types of committee to which a question may be referred? **RONR 173-74**
13-8	A.	The methods for appointing a committee.
	Q.	What are election by ballot; nominations from the floor with viva voce election; nominations by the chair; and appointment by the chair? **RON**
13-9	A.	Considered the chairman of the committee.
	Q.	What is who is the first named person to a committee? **RONR 175-76**
13-10	A.	The power to fill a vacancy in a committee.
	Q.	What is the appointing power? **RONR 177**

Section 14 – Postpone to a Certain Time (or Definitely)

Robert's Rules of Order Newly Revised, 11th Edition - Pages 179-91

14-1	A.	The motion used to delay consideration of a main motion until a specified later time.
	Q.	What is to Postpone to a Certain Time (or Postpone Definitely)? ***RONR 179***
14-2	A.	Amendable items in the motion Postpone to a Certain Time.
	Q.	What is time to which the main question can be postponed and whether or not it is a special order? ***RONR 182***
14-3	A.	A motion can be postponed to the next meeting (if held within the quarterly time interval) or to the end of the present session (if more than a quarterly time interval will elapse between meetings).
	Q.	What is the maximum time a motion can be postponed? ***RONR 183***
14-4	A.	When no more that a quarterly time interval will elapse between sessions, the question may not be postponed beyond this point.
	Q.	What is the next regular business session? ***RONR 183***
14-5	A.	Cannot be used to delay consideration of a class of subjects.
	Q.	What is when the motion Postpone to a Certain Time (or Definitely) cannot be used? ***RONR 184***
14-6	A.	A matter that the bylaws require to be business at a specified session can be postponed while it is pending to another session.
	Q.	What is by providing for an adjourned meeting? ***RONR 185***
14-7	A.	The name for a postponed item that becomes an item to be considered at a specified hour or after a particular event.
	Q.	What is a general order? ***RONR 186***
14-8	A.	The making of a postpone question a special order.
	Q.	What is when the motion Postpone To a Certain Time (or Definitely) requires a two-thirds vote? ***RONR 187***
14-9	A.	The name for a postponed item that usually becomes the immediately pending question at a certain time.
	Q.	What is "a special order"? ***RONR 187***
14-10	A.	The item of business which will be considered first at a meeting.
	Q.	What is "the special order"? ***RONR 187-88***

Section 15 – Limit or Extend Limits of Debate

Robert's Rules of Order Newly Revised, 11th Edition - Pages 191-97

15-1	A.	The motion that changes the rules on the number of times a person may speak to a question.
	Q.	What is Limit or Extend Limits of Debate? **RONR 191**
15-2	A.	The motion that changes the rules concerning the amount of time a person has to make a speech.
	Q.	What is Limit or Extend Limits of Debate? **RONR 191**
15-3	A.	The motion that will fix a time for debate to end and at which the vote will be taken.
	Q.	What is Limit or Extend Limits of Debate? **RONR 191**
15-4	A.	Type of motion Limit or Extend the Limits of Debate is when there is no other pending motion.
	Q.	What is an incidental main motion? **RONR 192**
15-5	A.	The subsidiary motions that takes precedence over all debatable motions.
	Q.	What are Limit or Extend Limits of Debate and Previous Question? **RONR 192**
15-6	A.	Motions that can be applied to the immediately pending question or an entire series of pending debatable motions.
	Q.	What are Limit or Extend Limits of Debate and Previous Question? **RONR 192**
15-7	A.	The vote required to adopt the motion Limit or Extend Limits of Debate.
	Q.	What is two-thirds? **RONR 193**
15-8	A.	Motions that cannot be adopted after adoption of a motion to close debate at a definite hour.
	Q.	What are to Commit or Refer and to Postpone to a Certain Time (or Postpone Definitely)? **RONR 194**
15-9	A.	Motions that can be applied to the immediately pending question and later applied to another pending question in the same series of motions.
	Q.	What are Limit or Extend Limits of Debate and Previous Question? **RONR 195**

Section 16 – Previous Question

Robert's Rules of Order Newly Revised, 11th Edition - Pages 197-209

16-1	A.	The motion, when adopted, that immediately closes debate and requires the assembly to vote.
	Q.	What is Previous Question? **RONR 197**
16-2	A.	The motion that prevents the making of any other subsidiary motion except Lay on the Table.
	Q.	What is Previous Question? **RONR 198**
16-3	A.	The motion that is not amendable but has the special characteristic that permits an effect similar to amendment when it is applied while a series of questions is pending.
	Q.	What is Previous Question? **RONR 200**
16-4	A.	The vote required to adopt Previous Question.
	Q.	What is two-thirds? **RONR 200**
16-5	A.	The effect of an interrupted order of Previous Question when the motion to Postpone to a Certain Time is adopted or a motion under that order is laid on the table and comes up again at the same session.
	Q.	What is continues to be in effect? **RONR 205**
16-6	A.	The time when an order of Previous Question is exhausted.
	Q.	What is when all the questions covered by the order have been voted on?
	Q.	What is when all the questions covered by the order have been resolved?
	Q.	What is the end of the session? **RONR 204**
16-7	A.	The effect of an interrupted order of Previous Question when the motion under that order is referred to a committee.
	Q.	What is the order is exhausted? **RONR 204**
16-8	A.	The effect of an interrupted order of Previous Question when a motion to Postponed to a Certain Time is adopted or a motion under that order is laid on the table and comes up again at the same session.
	Q.	What is continues to be in effect? **RONR 205**
16-9	A.	The effect of an adopted motion to Reconsider on the order of Previous Question.
	Q.	What is the presumed rejection of the motion Previous Question? **RONR 206**

Section 17 – Lay on the Table

Robert's Rules of Order Newly Revised, 11th Edition - Pages 209-18

17-1	A.	The motion which sets aside a main motion temporarily with no set time for resuming consideration.
	Q.	What is Lay on the Table? **RONR 209**
17-2	A.	The key requirement for use of the motion Lay on the Table.
	Q.	What is something else of immediate urgency? **RONR 209**
17-3	A.	The motion that is the highest in rank of all subsidiary motions.
	Q.	What is Lay on the Table? **RONR 210**
17-4	A.	Motions which can be laid on the table.
	Q.	What are main motions?
	Q.	What are debatable appeals that do not adhere? **RONR 210**
17-5	A.	The debatability status of the motion Lay on the Table.
	Q.	What is not debatable? **RONR 211**
17-6	A.	The vote required to lay a motion on the table.
	Q.	What is a majority? **RONR 212**
17-7	A.	The vote required to resume consideration of a motion laid on the table.
	Q.	What is a majority? **RONR 213**
17-8	A.	The rule concerning who can take a motion from the table.
	Q.	What is any member? **RONR 213**
17-9	A.	The condition of the motion and any adhering motions when taken from the table.
	Q.	What is the same condition as when laid on the table? **RONR 213**
17-10	A.	The time period when a motion laid on the table can be considered again.
	Q.	What is at the same meeting or before the adjournment of the next meeting (if held within the quarterly time interval)? **RONR 214**
17-11	A.	The status of a motion, which has been laid on the table, following the adjournment of the next meeting.
	Q.	What is it dies? **RONR 214**
17-12	A.	Motion often misused to kill a motion.
	Q.	What is Lay on the Table? **RONR 216**

CHAPTER VII: PRIVILEGED MOTIONS

Section 18 – Call for the Orders of the Day

Robert's Rules of Order Newly Revised, 11th Edition - Pages 219-24

18-1.	A.	The motion to require the assembly to conform to its agenda.	
	Q.	What is Call for the Orders of the Day?	**RONR 219**
18-2.	A.	The motion lowest in rank of the privileged motions.	
	Q.	What is Call for the Orders of the Day?	**RONR 220**
18-3.	A.	The number of members required to Call for the Orders of the Day.	
	Q.	What is one?	**RONR 221**
18-4.	A.	The vote required to set aside the Call for the Orders of the Day.	
	Q.	What is two-thirds in the negative?	**RONR 221**
18-5.	A.	The type of scheduled business which allows a Call for the Orders of the Day to interrupt pending business.	
	Q.	What is a special order?	**RONR 222**
18-6.	A.	A variation of committee where Call for the Orders of the Day is not allowed.	
	Q.	What is committee of the whole?	**RONR 222**
18-7	A.	Action of the chair when a Call for the Orders of the Day is made.	
	Q.	What is immediately announce the newly pending business?	**RONR 222**
18-8	A.	Action the chair can take when a Call for the Orders of the Day is made.	
	Q.	What is take a vote on proceeding with the orders of the day?	**RONR 223**
18-9	A.	Vote required to continue consideration of the pending question when the chair takes a vote on proceeding to the orders of the day.	
	Q.	What is a two-thirds vote in the negative?	**RONR 223**
18-10	A.	Action that can be taken by any member when Call for the Orders of the Day is made.	
	Q.	What is request that the time for consideration of the pending question be extended?	**RONR 223**
18-11	A.	Vote required to adopt the extension of time for consideration of the pending question when a Call for the Orders of the Day has been made.	
	Q.	What is a two-thirds vote in the affirmative?	**RONR 223**

Section 19 – Raise a Question of Privilege

Robert's Rules of Order Newly Revised, 11th Edition - Pages 224-30

19-1.	A.	The motion which permits a request or a main motion concerning the rights and privileges of the assembly or any of its members to be brought up.
	Q.	What is Raise a Question of Privilege? **RONR 224**
19-2	A.	The motion which permits the possible immediate consideration of an issue because of its urgency.
	Q.	What is Raise a Question of Privilege? **RONR 224**
19-3	A.	Action the chair takes after a member has stated his question of privilege.
	Q.	What is must rule on whether the request or motion is in fact a question of privilege? **RONR 225**
19-4	A.	Status of the request or motion raised by the motion Raise a Question of Privilege once admitted by the chair.
	Q.	What is handled as a request or treated as a main motion? **RONR 225**
19-5	A.	Cannot be interrupted by the motion Raise a Question of Privilege.
	Q.	What is voting or verification of a vote? **RONR 226**
19-6	A.	The two types of questions of privilege.
	Q.	What are questions of privilege relating to the assembly as a whole and questions of personal privilege? **RONR 227**
19-7	A.	Questions relating to the assembly's organization or existence; the comfort of its members; conduct of its officers; punishment of members; and accuracy of published reports.
	Q.	What are questions of privileges of the assembly? **RONR 227**
19-8	A.	Questions concerning incorrect record of member's participation; or charges circulated against a member's character.
	Q.	What are questions of personal privilege? **RONR 227**
19-9	A.	Status of the interrupted business when the action of Raise a Question of Privilege is completed.
	Q.	What is resumed at exactly the point at which it was interrupted? **RONR 228**

Section 20 - Recess

Robert's Rules of Order Newly Revised, 11th Edition - Pages 230-32

20-1	A.	The name applied to the motion calling for a short intermission in the assembly's proceedings.
	Q.	What is Recess? **RONR 230**
20-2	A.	Action commonly of only a few minutes and which does not close the meeting.
	Q.	What is a recess? **RONR 230**
20-3	A.	The status of business at the end of the recess.
	Q.	What is resumed at exactly the point where it was interrupted? **RONR 230**
20-4	A.	Action which can be taken while the ballots are being counted, while information is being secured, or to permit informal consultation.
	Q.	What is a recess? **RONR 230**
20-5	A.	When a recess is to begin immediately and while another question is pending.
	Q.	What is the privileged motion to Recess? **RONR 230**
20-6	A.	Condition under which the motion to Recess is privileged.
	Q.	What is only when another question is pending? **RONR 230-31**
20-7	A.	Time when a motion to recess at a future time is in order.
	Q.	What is only when no business is pending (as a main motion)? **RONR 230-31**
20-8	A.	Action of the chair when the time arrives for a recess scheduled in the adopted agenda.
	Q.	What is immediately announces the fact and declares the assembly in recess? **RONR 232**
20-9	A.	Action any member can take if a recess scheduled in an adopted agenda is missed by the chair.
	Q.	What is Call for the Orders of the Day? **RONR 232**
20-10	A.	The vote required to postpone a scheduled recess.
	Q.	What is two-thirds? **RONR 232**

21-1.	A.	The motion, if adopted, that will close the meeting.
	Q.	What is Adjourn? **RONR 233**

21-2	A.	The qualified motion to Adjourn.
	Q.	What is to adjourn at, or to, a future time?
	Q.	What is adjourning when the time has already been established?
	Q.	What is the motion Adjourn, if adopted, that will dissolve the assembly with no provision for another meeting such as in a convention? **RONR 234**

21-3	A.	The status of the motion to Adjourn made while the assembly is engaged in voting or verifying a vote.
	Q.	What is not in order? **RONR 235**

21-4	A.	The effect of adjournment on matters in the hands of a committee to which they have been referred during an annual session.
	Q.	What is remain with the committee? **RONR 237**

21-5	A.	The relationship of the motion to Adjourn and the making of important announcements.
	Q.	What is announcements are allowed while motion to Adjourn is pending and also allowed after the motion to Adjourn is adoption but before adjournment is announced? **RONR 238**

21-6	A.	Relationship of the motion to Adjourn and giving previous notice.
	Q.	What is giving notice of a motion to be made at the next meeting is allowed while the motion to Adjourn is pending and also after the motion to Adjourn is adoption but before adjournment is announced? **RONR 239**

21-7	A.	The action which actually closes the meeting.
	Q.	What is the chair's declaration that the meeting is adjourned? **RONR 239, 241**

21-8	A.	Situation where an assembly can adjourn without requiring the motion to Adjourn.
	Q.	What is when the time for adjournment has been prescheduled? **RONR 240**

Section 22 – Fix the Time to Which to Adjourn

Robert's Rules of Order Newly Revised, 11th Edition - Pages 242-46

22-1	A.	The motion, if adopted, that will establish a continuation of the present meeting.
	Q.	What is Fix the Time to Which to Adjourn? **RONR 242**
22-2	A.	In some cases, this may be included along with the time of the adjourned meeting, in the motion, Fix the Time to Which to Adjourn.
	Q.	What is the place of the meeting (when there is no fixed place for a meeting)? **RONR 242, 244**
22-3	A.	This is the effect of Fix Time to Which to Adjourn on the end of the current meeting.
	Q.	What is none? **RONR 242-45**
22-4	A.	The status of the motion to Fix the Time to Which to Adjourn when a meeting is already scheduled for later in the same session.
	Q.	What is out of order? **RONR 242**
22-5	A.	Time when the motion Fix a Time to Which to Adjourn is privileged.
	Q.	What is made when business in pending? **RONR 242**
22-6	A.	When the motion Fix the Time to Which to Adjourn is made when no business is pending.
	Q.	What is it is debatable and subject to all of the other rules applicable to main motions? **RONR 242-43**
22-7	A.	The privileged motion with highest precedence of all ranked motions.
	Q.	What is Fix the Time to Which to Adjourn? **RONR 243**
22-8	A.	These are the two subsidiary motions that may be applied to Fix the Time to Which to Adjourn as a privileged motion.
	Q.	What are Amend and Previous Question? **RONR 243**
22-9	A.	The motion which can be made while Fix the Time to Which to Adjourn is pending but cannot be considered.
	Q.	What is the motion to Reconsider? **RONR 243**
22-10	A.	The motion which can be moved even after the assembly has voted to adjourn, provided that the chair has not yet declared the assembly adjourned.
	Q.	What is Fix the Time to Which to Adjourn? **RONR 243**
22-11	A.	The condition for the time of an adjourned meeting established by the motion Fix the Time to Which to Adjourn.
	Q.	What is must be held before the next regularly scheduled meeting? **RONR 244**

22-12	A.	In this case, no time is fixed in the motion Fix the Time to Which to Adjourn.
	Q.	What is when the adjourned meeting is fixed to meet, "at the call of the chair?" **RONR 244**
22-13	A.	Status of the previous meeting when an adjourned meeting at the call of the chair us set if it isn't called.
	Q.	What is the adjournment of the previous session becomes final retrospectively as of the date the last meeting adjourned? **RONR 244**
22-14	A.	The status of the meeting established by the motion to Fix the Time to Which to Adjourn.
	Q.	What is a continuation of the present session? **RONR 244**
22-15	A.	Notice requirement for an adjourned meeting.
	Q.	What is none, although it is desirable? **RONR 244**
22-16	A,	Motions which frequently follow the adoption of the motion Fix the Time to Which to Adjourn.
	Q.	What is Postpone or to Adjourn? **RONR 244**
22-17	A.	Effect of the adoption of the motion Fix the Time to Which to Adjourn on the current meeting.
	Q.	What is none? **RONR 244-45**

CHAPTER VIII: INCIDENTAL MOTIONS

Section 23 - Point of Order

Robert's Rules of Order Newly Revised, 11th Edition - Pages 247-55

23-1	A.	The motion to use when a member thinks the rules of the assembly are being violated.
	Q.	What is Point of Order? **RONR 247**
23-2	A.	The subsidiary motion that can sometimes be made while a Point of Order, which adheres to pending question(s), is pending.
	Q.	What is to Lay on the Table? **RONR 247-48**
23-3	A.	The number of members required to raise a Point of Order.
	Q.	What is one? **RONR 247, 249**
23-4	A.	The vote required on a Point of Order.
	Q.	What is usually decided by the chair? **RONR 249**
23-5	A.	The time that a Point of Order is in order.
	Q.	What is immediately when the breach occurs? (see exception on page 251) **RONR 250**
23-6	A.	A motion adopted several months ago that conflicts with a provision of the bylaws, for example.
	Q.	What is a breach of a continuing nature? **RONR 251**
23-7	A.	Precedents are persuasive but not binding on the chair or the assembly.
	Q.	What is when similar issues arise in the future? **RONR 252**
23-8	A.	One or more members have been denied the right to vote.
	Q.	What is it is never too late to raise a point of order concerning the action taking in denying the basic rights of the individual members? **RONR 252**
23-9	A.	Things the chair can do before rendering his decision on a Point of Order.
	Q.	What is he can consult with the parliamentarian?
	Q.	What is he can request the advice of experienced members? **RONR 254**
23-10	A.	What the chair can do if he is in doubt on a Point of Order.
	Q.	What is submit it to the assembly for decision? **RONR 254**

Section 24 - Appeal

Robert's Rules of Order Newly Revised, 11ᵗʰ Edition - Pages 255-60

24-1	A.	The motion made when two members disagree with the ruling of the chair.	
	Q.	What is Appeal?	**RONR 255**
24-2	A.	If this wasn't done, members lose their right to criticize the ruling of the chair.	
	Q.	What is appeal?	**RONR 256**
24-3	A.	The ruling made on a Point of Order when another Point of Order is pending.	
	Q.	What is a ruling that cannot be appealed?	**RONR 256**
24-4	A.	The ruling on a question about which there cannot possibly be two reasonable opinions.	
	Q.	What is a ruling that cannot be appealed?	**RONR 256**
24-5	A.	Must be made at the time of the ruling.	
	Q.	What is when the motion to Appeal can be made?	**RONR 257**
24-6	A.	When the appeal relates to indecorum or a transgression of the rules of speaking; relates to the priority of business; or is made when an undebatable question is immediately pending or involved in the appeal.	
	Q.	What is when the motion to Appeal is undebatable?	**RONR 257**
24-7	A.	The special rules of debate on the motion Appeal.	
	Q.	What is members may speak only once but the chair, while remaining in the chair, may speak first and last?	**RONR 258**
24-8	A.	A majority vote or a tie vote sustains the decision of the chair.	
	Q.	What is the vote on the motion Appeal?	**RONR 258**
24-9	A.	The chair's opinion -- for example, his opinion on a parliamentary inquiry.	
	Q.	What is something that cannot be appealed?	**RONR 259**
24-10	A.	While this cannot be appealed, it can be challenged by calling for a Division?	
	Q.	What is the chair's announcement of the result of a vote?	**RONR 259**

Here is the Answer! What is the Question? Book 5

Robert's Rules of Order Newly Revised, 11th Edition - Pages 260-67

25-1	A.	The motion that allows the assembly to do something that it cannot do without violating one or more of its regular rules.
	Q.	What is Suspend the Rules? **RONR 260**
25-2	A.	Rules than cannot be suspended.
	Q.	What are bylaws (or constitution); local, state, or national laws prescribing applicable procedural rules; and fundamental principles of parliamentary law? **RONR 260**
25-3	A.	The usual vote to Suspend the Rules.
	Q.	What is two-thirds? **RONR 261**
25-4	A.	Condition under which a rule protecting a minority of a particular size cannot be suspended.
	Q.	What is in the face of a negative vote as large as the minority being protected? **RONR 261**
25-5	A.	The motion to take up a question out of its proper order.
	Q.	What is Suspend the Rules? **RONR 261**
25-6	A.	The motion to consider a motion that has been postponed before the time to which it has been postponed.
	Q.	What is Suspend the Rules? **RONR 261**
25-7	A.	An exception to the general rule that no member can make two motions at the same time except with the consent of the assembly.
	Q.	What is the combining of the motion Suspend the Rules and the making of the motion for which the rules are being suspended? **RONR 262**
25-8	A.	The vote requirement that allows the motion Suspend the Rules that was voted down to be made for the same purpose a second time at a meeting.
	Q.	What is unanimous consent? **RONR 262**
25-9	A.	Bylaws rule which can be suspended.
	Q.	What is only a rule that provides for its own suspension or is in the nature of a rule of order? **RONR 263**
25-10	A.	The rules may not be suspended so as to authorize cumulative voting.
	Q.	What is a fundamental principle that each member is entitled to one vote on a question? **RONR 263**

25-11	A.	Rules protecting a basic right of the individual member cannot be suspended.
	Q.	What is the right to attend meetings?
	Q.	What is the right to make motions or nominations?
	Q.	What is the right to speak in debate?
	Q.	What is the right to give previous notice?
	Q.	What is the right to vote? **RONR 264**
25-12	A.	Rules that have their application outside of the session which is in progress.
	Q.	What are rules that cannot be suspended? **RONR 264**
25-13	A.	Suspending the rules to permit postponement of a motion to a future session that will be held after the next regular business session or that will be held after more than a quarterly time interval has elapsed.
	Q.	What are not allowed? **RONR 265**
25-14	A.	Rules that can be suspended by a majority vote.
	Q.	What are ordinary standing rules? **RONR 265**
25-15	A.	Frequently used to suspend the rules for a non-controversial issue.
	Q.	What is unanimous consent? **RONR 266**

Section 26 – Objection to the Consideration of the Question

Robert's Rules of Order Newly Revised, 11th Edition - Pages 267-70

26-1	A.	The motion allows the assembly to avoid a particular original main motion altogether.
	Q.	What is Objection to the Consideration of a Question? ***RONR 267***
26-2	A.	The period of time when the motion Objection to the Consideration of a Question is in order.
	Q.	What is before any debate has begun or any subsidiary motion except Lay on the Table has been stated by the chair? ***RONR 267***
26-3	A.	The type of main motion to which Objection to the Consideration of a Question cannot be applied.
	Q.	What is an incidental main motion? ***RONR 268***
26-4	A.	Other than motions, things Objection to the Consideration of a Question can be applied to.
	Q.	What is petitions and correspondence that are not from a superior body? ***RONR 268***
26-5	A.	The vote required to sustain the objection raised by the making of the motion Object to the Consideration of a Question.
	Q.	What is two-thirds against consideration? ***RONR 268***
26-6	A.	Special rules for reconsidering Objection to the Consideration of a Question.
	Q.	What is the negative vote (the vote against consideration) can be reconsidered, but not an affirmative vote? ***RONR 268***
26-7	A.	Person who, on his own initiative, can make an Objection to the Consideration of a Question.
	Q.	Who is: the presiding officer, while in the chair? ***RONR 268***
26-8	A.	The effect of adoption of the motion Objection to the Consideration of a Question.
	Q.	What is dismissing the main motion for that session? ***RONR 269***
26-9	A.	The manner in which the motion Objection to the Consideration to a Question is put to a vote.
	Q.	What is "Shall the question be considered?" ***RONR 270***

Section 27 – Division of a Question

Robert's Rules of Order Newly Revised, 11th Edition - Pages 270-76

27-1	A.	The motion to separate a motion relating to a single subject into two or more parts.
	Q.	What is Division of a Question? **RONR 270**
27-2	A.	The attribute of a motion which can be divided.
	Q.	What is contains two or more parts which can stand alone?**RONR 270**
27-3	A.	When applied to a main motion, Division of a Question takes precedence over this subsidiary motion.
	Q.	What is Postpone Indefinitely? **RONR 271**
27-4	A.	Two subsidiary motions may be applied to Division of a Question.
	Q.	What are Amend and Previous Question? **RONR 271**
27-5	A.	Item which must be included in the motion Division of a Question.
	Q.	What is clear statement of the manner in which the question is to be divided? **RONR 272**
27-6	A.	More than one motion Division of a Question offering different divisions.
	Q.	What is permitted? **RONR 272**
27-7	A.	Each of the separated questions must be capable of standing alone.
	Q.	What is required in order to divide a question? **RONR 272**
27-8	A.	When a division of the question would require extensive rewriting of the separate parts.
	Q.	What is Division of a Question is NOT permitted? **RONR 272**
27-9	A.	The name for an amendment which is making the same adjustment to several places in the main motion.
	Q.	What is a conforming amendment? **RONR 273-74**
27-10	A.	The dividing of a conforming amendment.
	Q.	What is not permitted? **RONR 274**
27-11	A.	Action that can be taken to an undividable motion to eliminate undesirable parts.
	Q.	What is the amendment to strike out those parts? **RONR 274**
27-12	A.	A demand other than Division of the Question which requires that a motion be divided on the request of one member.
	Q.	What is a series of independent motions offered as a single motion? **RONR 274-75**

Section 28 - Consideration by Paragraph or Seriatim

Robert's Rules of Order Newly Revised, 11th Edition - Pages 276-80

28-1	A.	The motion to consider a motion by parts or sections.
	Q.	What is Consideration by Paragraph or Seriatim? **RONR 276**
28-2	A.	The rule of debate on a motion being considered by paragraph.
	Q.	What is right to debate begins again with the consideration of each paragraph? **RONR 277**
28-3	A.	The motion which is the opposite of the motion Consideration by Paragraph or Seriatim.
	Q.	What is considered as a whole? **RONR 278**
28-4	A.	The point in consideration when a new paragraph can be inserted.
	Q.	What is following consideration of all of the existing paragraphs? **RONR 278**
28-5	A.	The method of voting on a motion considered by paragraph.
	Q.	What is a single vote on the total motion? **RONR 278-79**
28-6	A.	The effect of motion to Postpone Indefinitely, Commit, Postpone Definitely, or Lay on the Table on a motion being considered by paragraph.
	Q.	What is applies to the total motion? **RONR 279**
28-7	A.	The special method of applying the motion Postpone Indefinitely to a motion being considered by paragraph.
	Q.	What is not debated or voted on until completion of consideration of all existing paragraphs? **RONR 279**
28-8	A.	The taking up of the motions Commit, Postpone Definitely, or Lay on the Table when a motion is being considered by paragraph.
	Q.	What is taken up as they arise? **RONR 279**
28-9	A.	A motion that is being considered by paragraphs comes again before the assembly after being Postponed to a Certain Time or Laid on the Table.
	Q.	What is resumed at the point it was interrupted? **RONR 279**
28-10	A.	The motions that may be applied to amendments or to the entire document but not to the individual paragraphs while a question is being considered by paragraphs.
	Q.	What is Previous Question and Limit or Extend Limits of Debate? **RONR 279**

Section 29 - Division of the Assembly

Robert's Rules of Order Newly Revised, 11th Edition - Pages 280-82

29-1	A.	The motion used when a member doubts the result of a voice vote.
	Q.	What is Division of the Assembly? **RONR 280**
29-2	A.	Votes where Division of the Assembly is in order.
	Q.	What is any vote taken by either a voice vote or show of hands? **RONR 280**
29-3	A.	The method for retaking a vote when a Division of the Assembly has been called.
	Q.	What is a rising vote? **RONR 281**
29-4	A.	The number of members required to demand a Division of the Assembly.
	Q.	What is one? **RONR 281**
29-5	A.	The period of time when the motion Division of the Assembly is in order.
	Q.	What is from the moment the negative votes have been cast until the announcement of the result is complete, or immediately thereafter? **RONR 281**
29-6	A.	How the chair recognizes the member calling for a Division of the Assembly.
	Q.	What is the member does not need to be recognized? **RONR 281**
29-7	A.	The vote required to adopt the motion Division of the Assembly.
	Q.	What is none (a single member can demand)? **RONR 281**
29-8	A.	Person who can order a rising vote without a motion.
	Q.	Who is: the chair? **RONR 281-82**
29-9	A.	When it is clear there has been a full vote and there is no reasonable doubt as to which side is in the majority.
	Q.	What is when Division of the Assembly is dilatory? **RONR 282**
29-10	A.	The easiest way is to call out "Division!"
	Q.	What is how does a member move for Division of the Assembly? **RONR 282**

Section 30 - Motions Relation to Methods of Voting and the Polls

Robert's Rules of Order Newly Revised, 11th Edition - Pages 283-86

30-1	A.	Motions relating to voting are used when the desire is to obtain a vote by some means other than these three voting methods.
	Q.	What are voice votes, show of hands, and standing votes? ***RONR 283***
30-2	A.	This is another name for roll call votes.
	Q.	What is the yeas and nays? ***RONR 283***
30-3	A.	They are the people that count standing votes.
	Q.	Who are: tellers? ***RONR 283***
30-4	A.	This unusual form of voting involves a ballot, but not a secret one.
	Q.	What is a signed ballot? ***RONR 283***
30-5	A.	Motions related to voting yield to this subsidiary motion.
	Q.	What is Lay on the Table? ***RONR 283***
30-6	A.	The vote required to adopt a motion which establishes the method of voting on another motion.
	Q.	What is majority? ***RONR 284***
30-7	A.	The vote required to close the polls.
	Q.	What is two-thirds? ***RONR 284***
30-8	A.	This method is sometimes used to get a truer expression of the assembly's will.
	Q.	What is a vote by ballot? ***RONR 285***
30-9	A.	After the vote has been taken by one of those other methods or the assembly has ordered a counted vote.
	Q.	What is not in order to move that the vote be taken again? ***RONR 285***
30-10	A.	Motions applicable only with respect to ballot votes.
	Q.	What are motions relating to opening and the closing the polls? ***RONR 286***
30-11	A.	The usual, and recommended, method of closing the polls.
	Q.	What is done by the chair? ***RONR 286***
30-12	A.	The vote required to reopen the polls.
	Q.	What is majority? ***RONR 286***

Here is the Answer! What is the Question? Book 5

51

Section 31 - Motions Relating to Nominations

Robert's Rules of Order Newly Revised, 11th Edition - Pages 287-89

31-1	A.	Motions relating to nominations yield to this subsidiary motion.
	Q.	What is Lay on the Table? ***RONR 287***
31-2	A.	When a motion to close nominations is out of order.
	Q.	What is when a member attempting to make a nomination?***RONR 287***
31-3	A.	The vote required to close nominations.
	Q.	What is two-thirds? ***RONR 287***
31-4	A.	The vote required to reopen nominations.
	Q.	What is majority? ***RONR 287***
31-5	A.	A motion to prescribe a method for making nominations is not in order.
	Q.	What is when the nomination process is set forth in the bylaws (constitution, rules of order)? ***RONR 288***
31-6	A.	When several methods of nominations are suggested, they are usually treated as this type of procedure.
	Q.	What is filling blanks? ***RONR 288***
31-7	A.	The order in which various methods of nominations are considered?
	Q.	What is by the chair, from the floor, by committee, by ballot, and by mail. ***RONR 288***
31-8	A.	The usual, and recommended, method to close nominations.
	Q.	What is done by the chair? ***RONR 288***
31-9	A.	A motion that is out of order when a member is trying to place a name into nomination.
	Q.	What is the motion to close nominations? ***RONR 288***
31-10	A.	This is a legitimate reason to close nominations even though someone wants to continue making them.
	Q.	What is when they are intended to honor persons that have no chance of being elected? ***RONR 289***

Section 32 - Request to Be Excused from a Duty

Robert's Rules of Order Newly Revised, 11th Edition - Pages 289-92

32-1	A.	Action which a member CANNOT take concerning a duty of membership.
	Q.	What is decline such a duty or demand but can request that he or she be relived from it? **RONR 289**
32-2	A.	Action which a member CAN take concerning a duty of membership.
	Q.	What is request from the assembly that he or she be excused from it? **RONR 289**
32-3	A.	Method by which a member requests the assembly to excuse him or her from a membership duty.
	Q.	What is by making the motion Request to Be Excused from a Duty? **RONR 289**
32-4	A.	The debatability status of the motion Request to Be Excused from a Duty.
	Q.	What is debatable? **RONR 290**
32-5	A.	The amendability status of the motion Request to Be Excused from a Duty.
	Q.	What is amendable? **RONR 290**
32-6	A.	The vote required to grant a Request to Be Excused from a Duty.
	Q.	What is a majority? **RONR 290**
32-7	A.	Action which a member can take when a duty is not compulsory.
	Q.	What is decline when he is first named to it? **RONR 290**
32-8	A.	Status of a member who remains silent when presumably aware that he has been named to a duty.
	Q.	What is regarded as accepting and thereby places himself under the same obligations as if he had expressly accepted? **RONR 290**
32-9	A.	The person who has the authority to receive a written resignation from an office, committee assignment, or other duty.
	Q.	What is the secretary or appointing power? **RONR 291**
32-10	A.	Action taken when a member in good standing with his dues paid submits his resignation.
	Q.	What is the resignation should be accepted immediately? **RONR 291-92**

Here is the Answer! What is the Question? Book 5

53

Robert's Rules of Order Newly Revised, 11th Edition - Pages 292-99

33-1	A.	The vote required for a Parliamentary Inquiry.
	Q.	What is none (answered by the chair)? **RONR 293**
33-2	A.	The vote on Request for Permission to Withdraw a Motion which can be reconsidered.
	Q.	What is only a negative vote? **RONR 293**
33-3	A.	A request for information concerning the parliamentary situation.
	Q.	What is Parliamentary Inquiry? **RONR 293-94**
33-4	A.	A request for factual information concerning the pending motion.
	Q.	What is Request for Information? **RONR 294**
33-5	A.	The time in debate is charged to speaker.
	Q.	What is when the speaker agrees to an inquiry? **RONR 295**
33-6	A.	The motion to withdraw a motion after it is has been stated by the chair.
	Q.	What is the Request for Permission to Withdraw a Motion? **RONR 296**
33-7	A.	The reason that the maker of the motion cannot withdraw the motion without permission after it is stated by the chair.
	Q.	What is because the motion belongs to the assembly? **RONR 296**
33-8	A.	The situation when the motion Request for Permission to Withdraw a Motion requires a second.
	Q.	What is when the request is made by the maker of the original motion after the motion has been stated by the chair? **RONR 296-97**
33-9	A.	The requirement to permit a speaker to quote extensively from a document.
	Q.	What is permission for a Request to Read Papers? **RONR 298-99**
33-10	A.	The right of a member out of the room on business of the assembly during the reading of a paper.
	Q.	What is having no right to the paper being read again? **RONR 299**
33-11	A.	The general category covering requests like: to address remarks or to make a presentation while no motion is pending.
	Q.	What is Request for Any Other Privilege? **RONR 299**

CHAPTER IX: MOTIONS THAT BRING A QUESTION AGAIN BEFORE THE ASSEMBLY

Section 34 - Take from the Table

Robert's Rules of Order Newly Revised, 11th Edition - Pages 300-04

34-1	A.	The motion to make pending again a motion previously tabled.
	Q.	What is Take from the Table? **RONR 300**
34-2	A.	The time when a motion to Take from the Table can be made.
	Q.	What is when no other motion is pending? **RONR 300**
34-3	A.	Time limits for taking a motion from the table.
	Q.	What is end of the present session, or end of next session if it is held within a quarterly time interval? **RONR 301-02**
34-4	A.	The result of not taking a motion from the table within the time limits.
	Q.	What is the motion dies? **RONR 302**
34-5	A.	The status of a motion taken from the table.
	Q.	What is exactly as it was when laid on the table? **RONR 303**
34-6	A.	The status of the rights to debate of a member who has already spoken twice in debate when a question is taken from the table on the same day it was laid on the table.
	Q.	What is exhausted, the member cannot speak again? **RONR 303**
34-7	A.	The status of member's right to debate again when a motion is taken from the table on a day other than the day it was laid on the table.
	Q.	What is no notice is taken of speeches previously made and the member's right to debate is renewed? **RONR 303**
34-8	A.	The status of an adhering Previous Question if the motion is taken from the table on the same day it was laid on the table.
	Q.	What is not exhausted, the motion is pending? **RONR 303**
34-9	A.	The status of an adhering limit or extension of debate if the motion is taken from the table on the same day it was laid on the table.
	Q.	What is not exhausted, the motion is still in force? **RONR 303**

Robert's Rules of Order Newly Revised, 11th Edition - Pages 305-10

35-1	A.	The relationship of the motions to Rescind and to Amend Something Previously Adopted.
	Q.	What is two forms of same incidental main motion? **_RONR 305_**
35-2	A.	The motion to strike out an entire main motion adopted at some previous time.
	Q.	What is the motion Rescind? **_RONR 305_**
35-3	A.	The motion to change part of a main motion adopted at some previous time.
	Q.	What is Amend Something Previously Adopted? **_RONR 305_**
35-4	A.	The motion to substitute a different version of a previously adopted motion.
	Q.	What is Amend Something Previously Adopted? **_RONR 305_**
35-5	A.	The status of the main motion that is the subject of Rescind or Amend Something Previously Adopted.
	Q.	What is the motion must have been adopted? **_RONR 305_**
35-6	A.	The status of the main motion which is the subject of the motion to Rescind or Amend Something Previously Adopted.
	Q.	What is also open to debate? **_RONR 306_**
35-7	A.	The vote required for the adoption of a motion to Rescind or Amend Something Previously Adopted in a meeting of an assembly when previous notice was not provided.
	Q.	What is a two-thirds vote, or a vote of the majority of the entire membership? **_RONR 306_**
35-8	A.	The vote required for the adoption of a motion to Rescind or Amend Something Previously Adopted in a meeting of an assembly when previous notice was provided.
	Q.	What is a majority vote? **_RONR 306_**
35-9	A.	The vote required for the adoption of a motion to Rescind or Amend Something Previously Adopted in meeting of a committee when ample notice was not provided to all committee members who voted for the motion.
	Q.	What is a two-thirds vote? **_RONR 306-07_**
35-10	A.	The vote required for the adoption of a motion to Rescind or Amend Something Previously Adopted in meeting of a committee when previous notice was provided.
	Q.	What is a majority vote? **_RONR 306-07_**

35-11	A.	The vote required for the adoption of a motion to Rescind or Amend a provision of a constitution or bylaws.
	Q.	What are the stated requirements for amendment contained in the document? **RONR 307**

35-12	A.	The vote required to Rescind or Amend special rules of order.
	Q.	What is the requirement of previous notice and a two-thirds vote?
	Q.	What is the requirement of a vote of a majority of the entire membership? **RONR 307**

35-13	A.	The vote required to Rescind or Amend bylaws or constitution when the document contains no provisions provision relating to amendment.
	Q.	What is the requirement of previous notice and a two-thirds vote?
	Q.	What is the requirement of a vote of a majority of the entire membership without notice? **RONR 307**

35-14	A.	The maximum time after a main motion has been adopted when the motion to Rescind or Amend Something Previously Adopted is valid.
	Q.	What is unlimited? **RONR 307**

35-15	A.	The restriction on how the member voted on the main motion which allows him or her to make the motion to Rescind or Amend Something Previously Adopted.
	Q.	What is no restriction? **RONR 307**

35-16	A.	When Rescind or Amend Something Previously Adopted cannot be used.
	Q.	What is when the motion can be reached by calling up the motion to Reconsider? **RONR 308**

35-17	A.	The status of action which would prevent use of the motion to Rescind or to Amend Something Previously Adopted.
	Q.	What is action that has been carried out in such a way which is too late to undo? **RONR 308**

35-18	A.	The status of the motion to Rescind when the action was the acceptance of a resignation.
	Q.	What is out of order? **RONR 308**

35-19	A.	The motion Rescind and Expunge from the Minutes.
	Q.	What is the motion used to express strong disapproval of previous action recorded in the minutes? **RONR 310**

35-20	A.	The vote required to adopt the motion Rescind and Expunge from the Minutes.
	Q.	What is an affirmative vote of a majority of the entire membership? **RONR 310**

Section 36 - Discharge a Committee

Robert's Rules of Order Newly Revised, 11th Edition - Pages 310-15

36-1	A.	The motion used to stop a committee from further consideration of an item.
	Q.	What is Discharge a Committee? **RONR 310**
36-2	A.	This motion can be used by a committee to consider something referred to a subcommittee.
	Q.	What is Discharge a Committee? **RONR 310n**
36-3	A.	Debate on Discharge a Committee can go into this.
	Q.	What is the merits of the question referred to the committee? **RONR 311**
36-4	A.	The vote required to adopt a motion to Discharge a Committee.
	Q.	What is two-thirds, majority with previous notice, or majority of entire membership? **RONR 312**
36-5	A.	When the committee fails to report within prescribed time as instructed or when considering any partial report of the committee.
	Q.	What is times when committee can be discharged by a majority vote without notice? **RONR 312**
36-6	A.	The method to force a committee to report when no instruction as to the time of reporting was given to the committee.
	Q.	What is the adoption of a motion instructing it to report at a specified time? **RONR 313**
36-7	A.	The time when the motion to Discharge a Committee is not needed.
	Q.	What is when the committee has made its final report? **RONR 313**
36-8	A.	The effect of adopting the motion Discharge a Committee on a special committee.
	Q.	What is the committee ceases to exist? **RONR 313**
36-9	A.	The effect of adopting the motion Discharge a Committee on a standing committee.
	Q.	What is the committee continues to exist? **RONR 313**
36-10	A.	The status of a motion which was referred to a committee by the motion to Commit on the adoption of a motion to Discharge a Committee.
	Q.	What is the motion becomes automatically pending before the assembly? **RONR 313**

Section 37 - Reconsider

Robert's Rules of Order Newly Revised, 11th Edition - Pages 315-35

37-1	A.	The origin of the motion Reconsider.
	Q.	What is American origin? **RONR 315**
37-2	A.	The motion to bring back for further consideration a motion already disposed of.
	Q.	What is Reconsider? **RONR 315**
37-3	A.	To permit correction of hasty, ill-advised, or erroneous action.
	Q.	What is the purpose of the motion Reconsider? **RONR 315**
37-4	A.	The special qualification of the member who makes the motion to Reconsider.
	Q.	What is the member must have voted on the prevailing side? **RONR 315**
37-5	A.	The special qualification of the member in a meeting of a standing or special committee who makes the motion to Reconsider.
	Q.	What is must have voted on the prevailing side or who did not vote at all? **RONR 315**
37-6	A.	The member who can make the motion to Reconsider when the motion was adopted by unanimous consent.
	Q.	What is any member present at the time of adoption? **RONR 316**
37-7	A.	Action of a member who did not vote on the prevailing side but believes there are valid reasons for the making of the motion to Reconsider.
	Q.	What is try to persuade someone who voted on the prevailing side to make the motion? **RONR 316**
37-8	A.	The time limit for making the motion to Reconsider in sessions of one day.
	Q.	What is can be made only on the same day the vote was taken? **RONR 316**
37-9	A.	The time limit for making the motion to Reconsider in sessions of more than one day.
	Q.	What is can be made only on same day the original vote was taken or next succeeding day within the session on which a business meeting is held? **RONR 316**
37-10	A.	The making of this motion has higher rank than its consideration.
	Q.	What is Reconsider? **RONR 316**

| 37-11 | A. | The effect of making the motion to Reconsider on the motion it is proposing to reconsider. |
| | Q. | What is the suspension of any action growing out of the vote on the motion proposed for reconsideration? **RONR 317** |

| 37-12 | A. | The action to consider the motion to Reconsider which could not be taken up when it was first made. |
| | Q. | What is calling up the motion to Reconsider? **RONR 317** |

| 37-13 | A. | The time limits for withdrawing a motion to Reconsider. |
| | Q. | What is same time limits as for making the motion in the first place? **RONR 317** |

| 37-14 | A. | The precedence of the making of the motion to Reconsider. |
| | Q. | What is over any other motion except Reconsider and Enter on the Minutes? **RONR 317n** |

| 37-15 | A. | The rank of the consideration of the motion to Reconsider. |
| | Q. | What is same rank as the motion to be reconsidered? **RONR 318** |

37-16	A.	The motion Reconsider can be applied to the vote on any motion except.
	Q.	What is a motion which can be renewed within a reasonable time?
	Q.	What is a negative vote that would be out of order because (i) it conflicts with a motion previously adopted and still in force, (ii) it conflicts with a motion which has been temporarily but not finally disposed of and which remains within the control of the assembly, or (iii) it would conflict with a pending motion if that motion were adopted?
	Q.	What is an affirmative vote whose provision have been partly carried out?
	Q.	What is an affirmative vote in the nature of a contract when the party to the contract has been notified of the outcome?
	Q.	What is any vote which has caused something to be done that it is impossible to undo?
	Q.	What is a vote on the motion to Reconsider?
	Q.	What is when practically the same result can be obtained by some other parliamentary motion? **RONR 318-19**

| 37-17 | A. | The time when the motion to Reconsider is seconded. |
| | Q. | What is when made, not when it is called up? **RONR 320** |

| 37-18 | A. | The special requirement for the member who seconds a motion to Reconsider. |
| | Q. | What is none? **RONR 320** |

| 37-19 | A. | The status of debate on the merits of the question proposed for reconsideration when motion to Reconsider is being debated. |
| | Q. | What is open to debate? **RONR 320** |

37-20 A.	The vote required to reconsider a motion requiring a two-thirds vote to adopt.	
Q.	What is majority?	**RONR 320**
37-21 A.	The status of action resulting from the vote on the motion proposed for reconsideration after the motion to Reconsider is made and before it is taken up.	
Q.	What is suspended?	**RONR 321**
37-22 A.	The time limits for the calling up of the motion to Reconsider after it is made.	
Q.	What is end of the present session or the end of the next session if held within a quarterly time interval?	**RONR 321**
37-23 A.	This terminates the suspension caused by the making of a motion to Reconsider.	
Q.	What is the completion of consideration of the motion reconsidered or when motion to Reconsider expires?	**RONR 321**
37-24 A.	The effect of the expiration or the time limits on the motion to Reconsider.	
Q.	What is as if Reconsider had never been made?	**RONR 321**
37-25 A.	The right of a member on the motion to Reconsider that is separate from the consideration of the motion proposed to be reconsidered.	
Q.	What is the right to debate?	**RONR 322**
37-26 A.	The action required to call up the motion to Reconsider.	
Q.	What is the request of a single member?	**RONR 323**
37-27 A.	The member who usually calls up a motion to Reconsider.	
Q.	What is the member who made the motion to Reconsider?	**RONR 323**
37-28 A.	The pointing out of the failure to call up a motion to Reconsider when harm may be done.	
Q.	What is the duty of the Chair?	**RONR 324**
37-29 A.	The status of the motion when a motion to Reconsider which was applied to it is adopted.	
Q.	What is the exact position it occupied the moment before it was voted on originally?	**RONR 324**
37-30 A.	The right to debate the original motion when a motion to Reconsider is adopted on a later day than when the vote on the original motion was taken.	
Q.	What is every member's right to debate begins again?	**RONR 325**

37-31	A.	The effect of debate on the motion to Reconsider when the motion proposed to be reconsidered was under an order limiting debate.
	Q.	What is those same limits continue to apply to debate? **RONR 325**
37-32	A.	The effect of debate on the motion to Reconsider when the motion proposed to be reconsidered was under an order extending limits of debate.
	Q.	What is those limits do not apply to the motion to Reconsider, but if reconsider is adopted those same limits apply once again to debate on the motion being reconsidered? **RONR 325**
37-33	A.	Situation when no other motions that would take precedence over the motion proposed to be reconsidered are also pending.
	Q.	What is Reconsider becomes the immediately pending question? **RONR 326**
37-34	A.	If in a series of motions Reconsider is applied to one of lower rank.
	Q.	What is motions of higher rank than the motion to which Reconsider is applied are considered first? **RONR 326-27**
37-35	A.	When reconsideration of a primary amendment is moved while another primary amendment is pending.
	Q.	What is completion of the pending primary amendment prior to the consideration of the motion to Reconsider? **RONR 327**
37-36	A.	The rule allowing debate on a subsidiary or incidental motion that is being reconsidered.
	Q.	What is debate on the subsidiary or incidental motion proposed to be reconsidered but not on any other pending motion? **RONR 327**
37-37	A.	The rule for reconsideration of an adhering subsidiary or incidental motion after the main motion has been adopted.
	Q.	What is the reconsideration of the main motion and the adhering subsidiary or incidental motion? **RONR 327-28**
37-38	A.	The motion Reconsider should be made to cover both the vote on the subsidiary or incidental motion and the vote on the main motion.
	Q.	What is the procedure for making the motion Reconsider when it is to apply to the main motion and adhering subsidiary or incidental motions after the main question has been acted on? **RONR 327-28**
37-39	A.	The member who can make the motion Reconsider when it is applied to a subsidiary or incidental motion and a main motion.
	Q.	What is the member who voted on the prevailing side on the subsidiary or incidental motion? **RONR 328**

| 37-40 | A. | The rule of debate when the motion Reconsider covers the vote on two or more connected motions such as a primary and secondary amendment. |
| | Q. | What is debate occurs only on the motion that will be voted on first if the motion Reconsider is adopted? **RONR 328** |

| 37-41 | A. | The time limits for making and taking up the motion to Reconsider in a committee. |
| | Q. | What is no time limits? **RONR 329** |

| 37-42 | A. | The limit on number of times a question can be reconsidered in a committee. |
| | Q. | What is unlimited? **RONR 329** |

| 37-43 | A. | The requirement for a member to make the motion to Reconsider in a committee. |
| | Q. | What is a member who didn't vote on the losing side? **RONR 330** |

| 37-44 | A. | The vote required in a committee to adopt the motion Reconsider unless all members who voted on the prevailing side are present or have been notified. |
| | Q. | What is a two-thirds vote? **RONR 330** |

| 37-45 | A. | The motion used to prevent a temporary majority from taking advantage of an unrepresentative attendance. |
| | Q. | What is Reconsider and Enter on the Minutes? **RONR 332** |

| 37-46 | A. | The time limit on when the motion Reconsider and Enter on the Minutes can be called up. |
| | Q. | What is cannot be called up on the day that it is made except when moved on the last day (but not the last meeting) of the session? **RONR 334** |

| 37-47 | A. | The rank of the motion Reconsider and Enter on the Minutes relative to the motion Reconsider. |
| | Q. | What is higher (takes precedence over)? **RONR 333** |

37-48	A.	The vote to which the motion Reconsider and Enter on the Minutes can be applied.
	Q.	What is the vote that finally disposes of a main motion?
	Q.	What is an affirmative vote on the motion Postpone Indefinitely?
	Q.	What is a negative vote on the motion Objection to Consideration of a Question? **RONR 333-34**

| 37-49 | A. | The only time the motion Reconsider and Enter on the Minutes can be called up on the same day it is made. |
| | Q. | What is the last day of a session when the next session to be held is more than a quarterly time interval away? **RONR 334** |

CHAPTER X: RENEWAL OF MOTIONS;
DILATORY AND IMPROPER MOTIONS

Section 38 – Renewal of Motions

Robert's Rules of Order Newly Revised, 11th Edition - Pages 336-42

38-1	A.	A term used to denote a motion which was disposed of without being adopted and is again before the assembly.
	Q.	What is renewed? **RONR 336**
38-2	A.	Basic principle for the limitation on renewal of motions.
	Q.	What is an assembly cannot be asked to decide the same, or substantially the same, question twice during one session? **RONR 336**
38-3	A.	Two motions used to cause the assembly to consider a question for a second time during the session.
	Q.	What is to reconsider the vote or to rescind an action? **RONR 336**
38-4	A.	When a motion has significant change in wording or when there is change in time or circumstances in the meeting in which it is proposed.
	Q.	What is times when a motion may be renewed? **RONR 336**
38-5	A.	Restrictions of renewal relative to a motion withdrawn earlier.
	Q.	What is none? **RONR 336**
38-6	A.	A motion made but not seconded.
	Q.	What is can be renewed? **RONR 337**
38-7	A.	The rule concerning making the same motion again at the same session.
	Q.	What is cannot be renewed unless it becomes essentially a different question? **RONR 337**
38-8	A.	The rule concerning making the same motion at the next session.
	Q.	What is the motion can be renewed? **RONR 337**
38-9	A.	Renew status of a resolution which was lost when voted on a part of a series of resolutions.
	Q.	What is can be offered again? **RONR 338**
38-10	A.	The rule concerning renewal of the motion Postpone Indefinitely in connection with the same main motion during the same session.
	Q.	What is cannot be renewed? **RONR 338**

| 38-11 | A. | The rule concerning renewal of a rejected motion to *Reconsider* in connection with the same vote. |
| | Q. | What is cannot be renewed? **RONR 338** |

| 38-12 | A. | The rule concerning proposing to divide the same question substantially in the same way. |
| | Q. | What is cannot be renewed? **RONR 338** |

| 38-13 | A. | The rule concerning the renewal of a Question of Privilege or a Point of Order that has been ruled on adversely by the chair. |
| | Q. | What is cannot be renewed during the same session unless an appeal is made and the chair's decision is reversed? **RONR 338-39** |

| 38-14 | A. | The rule concerning the renewal of an Appeal involving the same principles during the same session. |
| | Q. | What is cannot be renewed? **RONR 339** |

| 38-15 | A. | The general rule for renewal of Call for the Orders of the Day. |
| | Q. | What is after disposal of the business that was taken up when the assembly refused to proceed to the orders of the day? **RONR 340** |

| 38-16 | A. | The rule for renewal of Adjourn or to Recess. |
| | Q. | What is after material progress in business or debate? **RONR 340** |

| 38-17 | A. | When motions to close or to reopen nominations can be renewed. |
| | Q. | What is after sufficient progress in nominations or debate to make the motion a new question? **RONR 340** |

| 38-18 | A. | Method where a main motion remains within the control of the assembly while being carried over to a later session. |
| | Q. | What is referred to a committee? **RONR 341** |

| 38-19 | A. | The incidental motion which, if not adopted, cannot be renewed. |
| | Q. | What is Objection to the Consideration of a Question? **RONR 341-42** |

Section 39 - Dilatory and Improper Motions

Robert's Rules of Order Newly Revised, 11th Edition - Pages 342-44

39-1	A.	A motion that seeks to obstruct or thwart the will of the assembly.
	Q.	What is a motion that is dilatory? **RONR 342**
39-2	A.	The right to protect itself from the dilatory use of parliamentary forms.
	Q.	What is a right of every deliberative assembly? **RONR 342**
39-3	A.	A main or other motion that is frivolous or absurd or contains no rational proposition.
	Q.	What is a motion that is dilatory? **RONR 342**
39-4	A.	Appealing from a ruling of the chair on a question about which there cannot possibly be two reasonable opinions.
	Q.	What is an action considered dilatory? **RONR 342**
39-5	A.	Demanding a division on a vote even when there has been a full vote and the result is clear.
	Q.	What is an action considered dilatory? **RONR 342**
39-6	A.	Moving to lay on the table the matter for which a special meeting has been called.
	Q.	What is an action considered dilatory? **RONR 342**
39-7	A.	Constantly raising points of order and appealing from the chair's decisions on them.
	Q.	What is an action considered dilatory? **RONR 342**
39-8	A.	Moving to adjourn again and again when nothing has happened to justify renewal of such a motion.
	Q.	What is an action considered dilatory? **RONR 342**
39-9	A.	To prevent members from misusing the legitimate forms of motions merely to obstruct business.
	Q.	What is the duty of the presiding officer? **RONR 342**
39-10	A.	The recourse the chair has when he becomes convinced that one or more members are using parliamentary forms for obstructive purposes.
	Q.	What is should not recognize members or should rule their motions out of order? **RONR 342-43**
39-11	A.	A motion which conflicts with the corporate charter, constitution, bylaws, or other rules of a society.
	Q.	What is an improper motion that is out of order? **RONR 343**

39-12	A.	A motion which is in conflict with a motion adopted at a previous session and has not been rescinded.
	Q.	What is an improper motion that is out of order? **RONR 343**
39-13	A.	A motion which presents practically the same question as a motion previously decided in the same session.
	Q.	What is a motion that is out of order? **RONR 343**
39-14	A.	A motion which conflicts with a motion that is within the control of the assembly.
	Q.	What is an improper motion that is out of order? **RONR 343**
39-15	A.	The requirement in order to introduce a motion outside the object of the society.
	Q.	What is a two-thirds vote agreeing to consideration? **RONR 343-44**
39-16	A.	Except in special cases, a motion which uses language not allowed in debate.
	Q.	What is not allowed (out of order)? **RONR 344**
39-17	A.	An exception to the rule that a motion must not use language not allowed in debate.
	Q.	What is a motion to censure or a motion relative to disciplinary procedures? **RONR 344**
39-18	A.	An exception to the rule that a motion must not use language not allowed in debate.
	Q.	What is a motion to censure or a motion relative to disciplinary procedures? **RONR 344**

CHAPTER XI: QUORUM; ORDER OF BUSINESS AND RELATED CONCEPTS

Section 40 - Quorum

Robert's Rules of Order Newly Revised, 11th Edition - Pages 345-51

40-1	A.	The number of members who must be present in order that business can be validly transacted.	
	Q.	What is the definition of quorum?	**RONR 345**
40-2	A.	The place where information is found on the quorum for an assembly.	
	Q.	What is the organization's bylaws?	**RONR 345**
40-3	A.	The quorum for a mass meeting.	
	Q.	What is the number of persons present at the time?	**RONR 345**
40-4	A.	The quorum for a meeting of a church or other organization where there is no required or effective annual dues and the register of members is not generally reliable as a list of the bona fide members.	
	Q.	What is those who attend?	**RONR 346**
40-5	A.	The quorum of a body of delegates such as a convention.	
	Q.	What is a majority of the number who have been registered as attending?	**RONR 346**
40-6	A.	The quorum of an organization with an enrolled membership whose bylaws do not specify one.	
	Q.	What is a majority of the members?	**RONR 346**
40-7	A.	Suggested size of the quorum in a voluntary society with an enrolled membership.	
	Q.	What is relatively small, considerably less than a majority?	**RONR 346**
40-8	A.	Method of specifying the quorum which is not recommended.	
	Q,	What is a percentage of the membership?	**RONR 346**
40-9	A.	The quorum should be as large a number of members as can reasonably be depended on to be present at any meeting, except in very bad weather or other exceptionally unfavorable conditions.	
	Q.	What is how should an organization determine the quorum to be specified in the bylaws?	**RONR 346**
40-10	A.	The proper procedure for changing the quorum in the bylaws which is made and voted on as one question.	
	Q.	What is to strike out the old provision and insert the new provision?	**RONR 346-47**

40-11	A.	The quorum for a committee of the whole or its variations.
	Q.	What is same as in the assembly unless specified otherwise?
		RONR 347

40-12	A.	The quorum of a board or committee unless the bylaws specify otherwise.
	Q.	What is a majority of the members? **RONR 347**

40-13	A.	Status of actions, except for certain specified ones, taken in the absence of a quorum.
	Q.	What is null and void? **RONR 347**

40-14	A.	The only actions that can be taken are: to Fix the Time to Which to Adjourn, Adjourn, Recess, take measures to obtain a quorum, and certain procedural motions.
	Q.	What is actions that can be taken in the absence of a quorum?
		RONR 347

40-15	A.	Availability of subsidiary and incidental motions and some others in the absence of a quorum.
	Q.	What is only if they are related to the three motions permitted or to the conduct of the meeting while it remains without a quorum?
		RONR 347-48

40-16	A.	A motion that absent members be contacted during a recess at a meeting without a quorum.
	Q.	What is is allowed? **RONR 348**

40-17	A.	Status of a motion to obtain a quorum at a meeting without a quorum.
	Q.	What is a main motion when no business is pending or as a privileged motion which takes precedence over a motion to recess?**RONR 3**

40-18	A.	The prohibition of transacting business in the absence of a quorum.
	Q.	What is cannot be waived even by unanimous consent? **RONR 348**

40-19	A.	When the members present take action informally in the absence of a quorum.
	Q.	What is taken at the risk of those present? **RONR 348**

40-20	A.	The situation when action is taken in the absence of a quorum.
	Q.	What is can be ratified at a later meeting? **RONR 348**

40-21	A.	Action that a committee of the whole must take if it finds itself without a quorum.
	Q.	What is rise and report to the assembly? **RONR 348**

40-22	A.	Action concerning a quasi committee of the whole if it finds itself without a quorum.
	Q.	What is quasi committee is ended? **RONR 348**
40-23	A.	If a quorum is not present at the time for the meeting to be called to order, the action that should be taken by the presiding officer.
	Q.	What is waits a reasonable time for a quorum to appear? **RONR 349**
40-24	A.	The chair calls the meeting to order, announces the absence of a quorum, and entertains a motion to adjourn or one of the other motions allowed.
	Q.	What is the duties of the chair when a quorum is not present following waiting a reasonable time? **RONR 349**
40-25	A.	While conducting business, the status that is presumed even when some members leave prior to adjournment.
	Q.	What is the continued presence of a quorum? **RONR 349**
40-26	A.	Declares the absence of a quorum, at least before taking any vote or stating the question on any new motion.
	Q.	What is a duty of the chair when he notices the absence of a quorum? **RONR 349**
40-27	A.	Action a member can take when he notices the apparent absence of a quorum.
	Q.	What is to raise a point of order but not to interrupt a speaker during debate? **RONR 349**
40-28	A.	Action on a pending question which can continue in the absence of a quorum.
	Q.	What is debate? **RONR 349**
40-29	A.	Not permitted to affect prior action unless there is clear and convincing proof which proves as to when a quorum ceased to exist.
	Q.	What is a point of order relating to the absence of a quorum? **RONR 349**
40-30	A.	Used in legislative bodies or other such assemblies to compel attendance of their members.
	Q.	What is Call of the House? **RONR 350**
40-31	A.	Unexcused absent members can be brought to the meeting under arrest.
	Q.	What is action under a Call of the House? **RONR 350**

40-32 A. Motions allowed after adoption of a call of the house until a quorum is present.
Q. What is none except those relating to the call? **RONR 351**

Here is the Answer! What is the Question? Book 5

71

Section 41 - Order of Business; Orders of the Day; Agenda or Program

Robert's Rules of Order Newly Revised, 11th Edition - Pages 351-75

41-1	A.	Order of business, orders of the day, agenda, and program.	
	Q.	What is closely related concepts having to do with the order in which business is taken up in a session?	**RONR 351**
41-2	A.	Any established sequence which may prescribe the order in which business shall be taken up at a session of a given assembly.	
	Q.	What is an order of business?	**RONR 351**
41-3	A.	An order of business that specifies the general classes of business and gives only the order in which they are to be taken up is found here.	
	Q.	What is in the rules of the organization?	**RONR 351**
41-4	A.	An order of business expressly adopted for a particular session containing assigned positions, and even times, to specific items for business.	
	Q.	What is an agenda or program?	**RONR 351-52**
41-5	A.	Prescribed items of business of an entire session.	
	Q.	What is an order of business, an agenda, or a program?	**RONR 352**
41-6	A.	An item of business that is prescheduled to be taken up at that meeting.	
	Q.	What is an order of the day?	**RONR 352**
41-7	A.	The two classes of orders of the day.	
	Q.	What are general orders and special orders?	**RONR 352**
41-8	A.	Unless designated for particular hours, general orders and special orders are usually taken up this way.	
	Q,	What is under the assigned headings in the order of business?	**RONR 352**
41-9	A.	Point in the meeting when the order of business comes into play.	
	Q.	What is following the call to order and any customary opening ceremonies?	**RONR 354**
41-10	A.	The phrase used by the chair in requesting the secretary to read the minutes.	
	Q.	What is "The secretary will read the minutes?"	**RONR 354**
41-11	A.	Allowed when the minutes are sent to all members in advance.	
	Q.	What is reading of the minutes aloud may be omitted unless any member requests that they be read?	**RONR 354**

41-12	A.	The situation when there are minutes of other than the previous meeting that have not been approved.
	Q.	What is they are processed in order of date from earliest to latest? **RONR 354**

41-13	A.	The phrase used by the chair to seek corrections to the minutes.
	Q.	What is "Are there any corrections to the minutes?" **RONR 354**

41-14	A.	Usual method of handling corrections to the minutes.
	Q.	What is by unanimous consent? **RONR 354**

41-15	A.	"If there are no corrections (or "no further corrections"), the minutes stand (or "are") approved (or "approved as read," or "approved as corrected")."
	Q.	What is the phrase used by the chair stating the assembly's approval of the minutes? **RONR 354-55**

41-16	A.	Status of the draft of the minutes the members receive before or at the meeting.
	Q,	What is may become inaccurate copies of the approved minutes? **RONR 355**

41-17	A.	Time when the minutes assumed their status as the official record of the proceedings.
	Q.	What is when the minutes are approved? **RONR 355**

41-18	A.	Officer and committee reports which the chair should call for.
	Q.	What is only those who have reports to make? **RONR 355**

41-19	A.	The order of calling for reports of standing committees.
	Q.	What is the order listed in the bylaws? **RONR 356**

41-20	A.	The person who should make the motion when an officer's reports contains a recommendation.
	Q.	Who is: another member and not the officer? **RONR 356**

41-21	A.	The person who should make the motion when a committee report contains a recommendation.
	Q.	Who is: the reporting member? **RONR 356**

41-22	A.	Time when a recommendation in an officer or committee report is handled.
	Q.	What is taken up immediately? **RONR 356**

41-23	A.	Situation for an item of business from the class of officer and standing committee reports which was laid on the table at the previous meeting.
	Q.	What is can be taken from the table under this heading? **RONR 356**

41-24	A.	The order in which they were appointed and only those prepared or were instructed to report.
	Q.	What is the order for calling for reports of special committees? **RONR 356**

41-25	A.	Situation for business relative to special committees that is on the table.
	Q.	What is may be taken from the table under this heading? **RONR 356**

41-26	A.	Place in the order of business where an unfinished special order should be handled.
	Q.	What is under the heading of special orders? **RONR 356-57**

41-27	A.	The order of handling any special orders from the previous meeting.
	Q.	What is starting with the one pending at the adjournment of the previous meeting and continuing in the order in which they were made? **RONR 356-57**

41-28	A.	Other items of business to be considered under the heading of special orders.
	Q.	What is items made special orders for the present meeting without being set for specific hours? **RONR 357**

41-29	A.	Not required for an order of the day unless it was made as a part of an agenda for a session.
	Q.	What is no motion is needed when the order comes up? **RONR 357**

41-30	A.	The place in an order of business when items required by the bylaws to be considered at a particular meeting are taken up.
	Q.	What is special orders? **RONR 357**

41-31	A.	When there is not more than a quarterly time interval between regular meetings, item which come over from the previous meeting come under this class.
	Q.	What is unfinished business and general orders? **RONR 358**

41-32	A.	Name for the question that was pending when the previous meeting adjourned.
	Q.	What is unfinished business? **RONR 358**

41-33	A.	Name for a question that was scheduled as unfinished business at the previous meeting but not reached before adjournment.
	Q.	What is a question for this meeting's unfinished business? **RONR 358**

41-34	A.	Name for a question which, by postponement or otherwise, was set as a general order for the previous meeting and was not reached before it adjourned.
	Q.	What is unfinished business? **RONR 358**

41-35	A.	Business that can be taken up under the heading of General Orders.
	Q.	What is a motion that was postponed to or otherwise made a general order for the present meeting? **RONR 359**

41-36	A.	The phrase that the chair should not use when the heading of Unfinished Business and General Orders is reached.
	Q.	What is "Is there any unfinished business?" **RONR 359**

41-37	A.	Status of any item which has been laid on the table and the class of unfinished business and general orders has been reached.
	Q.	What is any tabled item can be taken from the table under this class? **RONR 359**

41-38	A.	The phrase the chair should use when calling for new business.
	Q.	What is "Is there any new business?" **RONR 360**

41-39	A.	Items of business which can be brought up during new business.
	Q.	What is any? **RONR 360**

41-40	A.	An invocation, the singing of the national anthem, etc.
	Q.	What are opening ceremonies or exercises? **RONR 360-61**

41-41	A.	The verification of the attendance of officers and sometimes members.
	Q.	What is a roll call? **RONR 361**

41-42	A.	A useful tool for disposing of large number of routine matters.
	Q.	What is a consent calendar? **RONR 361**

41-43	A.	A heading in an order of business that may be used for informal observations regarding the work of the organization.
	Q.	What is good of the order, general good and welfare, or open forum? **RONR 362**

41-44	A.	Items of information usually handled just prior to the program or adjournment.
	Q.	What are announcements? **RONR 362**

41-45	A.	Item which typically occurs after the order of business has been completed.
	Q.	What is the program? **RONR 362**

41-46	A.	Usual method to take up an item out of its proper order.
	Q.	What is suspend the rules by a two-thirds vote or unanimous consent? **RONR 363**

| 41-47 | A. | Method that can be used to take up an item out of its proper order when only one or two items stand ahead of the item it is desired to reach. |
| | Q. | What is lay the intervening items on the table individually or to postpone them as they arise? **RONR 363** |

| 41-48 | A. | To lay on the table or postpone a class of items. |
| | Q. | What is not in order? **RONR 363** |

| 41-49 | A. | A particular subject, question, or item of business that is set in advance to be taken up during a given session, day, or meeting, or at a given hour. |
| | Q. | What is an order of the day? **RONR 364** |

| 41-50 | A. | Time beyond which an order of the day cannot be made when the next regular business session of the organization is more than a quarterly time interval. |
| | Q. | What is the end of the present session? **RONR 364** |

| 41-51 | A. | Time beyond which an order of the day cannot be made when the next regular business session of the organization is within a quarterly time interval. |
| | Q. | What is the end of that next session? **RONR 364** |

| 41-52 | A. | A special order set for a particular hour when that hour arrives. |
| | Q. | What is interrupts any pending business? **RONR 365** |

| 41-53 | A. | The vote required to make a special order. |
| | Q. | What is two-thirds? **RONR 365** |

| 41-54 | A. | Term for the postponement of a pending motion to a specified time, or the postponement of a not yet pending motion to a future time, or the specific position of an item of business in an adopted agenda or program. |
| | Q. | What is an order of the day? **RONR 365** |

| 41-55 | A. | Motion used to prevent a matter from coming before the assembly until a future time. |
| | Q. | What is Postpone to a Certain Time (or Definitely)? **RONR 366** |

| 41-56 | A. | No other business is pending; the category of general orders has been reached; no special order interferes; no reconsideration interferes; and no general order made before this order remains undisposed. |
| | Q. | What is conditions that must be met before a general order can be considered? **RONR 368** |

41-57	A.	General orders taken up in the order they were made.
	Q.	What is how consideration of several general orders made for the same time are handled? **RONR 368**
41-58	A.	Special orders taken up in the order they were made.
	Q.	What is how consideration of several special orders made for the same time are handled? **RONR 369**
41-59	A.	The vote required to consider a special order prior to the established time.
	Q.	What is a two-thirds vote? **RONR 369**
41-60	A.	When it does not interfere with adjournment or recess; question of privilege; a special order made before it; or the special order.
	Q.	What is when a special order can be considered? **RONR 369**
41-61	A.	Situation when during consideration of a special order, the time scheduled for a recess or adjournment arrives.
	Q.	What is the recess or adjournment takes precedence? **RONR 370**
41-62	A.	The vote required to postpone a prescheduled recess or adjournment.
	Q.	What is two-thirds? **RONR 370**
41-63	A.	Takes up an entire meeting or as much of the meeting as necessary, for a subject to be considered.
	Q.	What is the special order for a meeting? **RONR 371**
41-64	A.	Order that is taken up as soon as the minutes are approved.
	Q.	What is the special order for a meeting? **RONR 371**
41-65	A.	A series of special orders or general orders or a mixture of both.
	Q.	What is an agenda? **RONR 371**
41-66	A.	Point in the session when the agenda is usually adopted.
	Q.	What is at the outset? **RONR 372**
41-67	A.	Vote required to adopt an agenda when the organization already has an order of business with which it does not conflict.
	Q.	What is a majority vote if it does not create any special orders? **RONR 372**
41-68	A.	Status of an agenda provided in advance.
	Q.	What is information only unless formally adopted? **RONR 372**
41-69	A.	Vote required to adjust an agenda when it is being considered for adoption.
	Q.	What is a majority? **RONR 373**

| 41-70 | A. | The vote required to change an adopted agenda or program. |
| | Q. | What is two-thirds, a majority of the entire membership, or unanimous consent? **RONR 373** |

| 41-71 | A. | Reconsideration of the vote adopting an agenda. |
| | Q. | What is not permitted? **RONR 373** |

| 41-72 | A. | One includes only items of business and the other also includes times for speakers, meals, and other non-business matters. |
| | Q. | What is difference between an agenda and a program? **RONR 373** |

| 41-73 | A. | Process when the assigned time for taking up a topic in the agenda arrives and there is business pending. |
| | Q. | What is chair announces topic and then calls for an immediate vote on the pending business? **RONR 373** |

| 41-74 | A. | Parliamentary conditions for a motion to extend consideration of the pending business when the time in the agenda for a topic arrives. |
| | Q. | What is motion to extend is not debatable and requires a two-thirds vote? **RONR 373** |

| 41-75 | A. | Happens when the time for a scheduled recess or adjournment arrives. |
| | Q. | What is chair immediately declares the recess or adjournment? **RONR 374** |

| 41-76 | A. | Item of business advisable to be included periodically or near the end of the agenda. |
| | Q. | What is provision for unfinished business? **RONR 374-75** |

| 41-77 | A. | Status of unfinished business items, which were scheduled for today in the agenda of a multi-day session. |
| | Q. | What is become the first items of business the next day? **RONR 375** |

CHAPTER XII: ASSIGNMENT OF THE FLOOR; DEBATE

Section 42 - Rules Governing Assignment of the Floor

Robert's Rules of Order Newly Revised, 11th Edition - Pages 376-85

42-1	A.	Required action before a member can make a motion or speak in debate.
	Q.	What is must be recognized by the chair? ***RONR 376***
42-2	A.	Recognize any member who seeks the floor when entitled to it.
	Q.	What is must be done by the chair? ***RONR 376-77***
42-3	A.	If only one person is seeking the floor in a small meeting where all present can clearly see one another.
	Q.	What is the chair may recognize the member by merely nodding to him? ***RONR 377***
42-4	A.	Words used by the chair in granting recognition in a large meeting.
	Q.	What is "The chair recognizes ..."? ***RONR 377***
42-5	A.	Words used by the chair in granting recognition at a time when the floor can be granted only for limited purposes.
	Q.	What is "For what purpose does the member rise?" or "For what purpose does the member address the chair?" ***RONR 377***
42-6	A.	A motion called out by anyone who has not obtained the floor.
	Q.	What is ignored by the chair? ***RONR 377***
42-7	A.	Entitled to be recognized when two or more members rise at about the same time to claim the floor.
	Q.	What is the member who rose and addressed the chair first after the floor was yielded is entitled to be recognized? ***RONR 378***
42-8	A.	Not entitled to the floor before it has been yielded unless the parliamentary situation warrants interruption.
	Q.	What is a member who rises before the floor has been yielded? ***RONR 378***
42-9	A.	Another member cannot rise to claim preference in recognition.
	Q.	What is after the chair has actually recognized a member? ***RONR 378***
42-10	A.	Immediately after chair reports a vote, a member making an appropriate motion that the vote be taken again by another method.
	Q.	What is a member with preference in recognition? ***RONR 378***

42-11	A.	Highest preference for recognition when a debatable motion is pending.
	Q.	What is to give previous notice? **RONR 379**
42-12	A.	Preference for the member who made the motion claims the floor and has not already spoken on the question when a debatable motion is pending.
	Q.	Who is: first except for one giving previous notice? **RONR 379**
42-13	A.	The person having preference in recognition in the case of a motion to implement a recommendation in a committee report.
	Q.	Who is: the reporting member? **RONR 379**
42-14	A.	The person having preference in recognition when a motion has just been taken from the table.
	Q.	Who is: the person moving the take from the table motion? **RONR 379**
42-15	A.	The person having preference in recognition when a motion of reconsideration has been called up.
	Q.	Who is: the person who made the motion of reconsideration, not the person who calls it up? **RONR 379**
42-16	A.	Any member who has not spoken on the pending question claims the floor has preference over.
	Q.	What is a member who has already spoken? **RONR 379**
42-17	A.	The chair should in situations where he knows that persons seeking the floor have opposite opinions.
	Q.	What is let the floor alternate, as far as possible, between those favoring and those opposing? **RONR 379-80**
42-18	A.	Has preference in the case of an appeal or a point of order submitted to a vote.
	Q.	Who is: the chair is entitled to speak once in preference and a second time at the close of the debate? **RONR 380**
42-19	A.	When a member has moved to reconsider the vote on a motion for the announced purpose of amending it.
	Q.	What is entitled to preference in recognition in order to move his amendment? **RONR 380**
42-20	A.	Preference in recognition when an undebatable question is immediately pending.
	Q.	What is granted to a member who wishes to make a motion of higher rank or wishes to give previous notice of a motion? **RONR 380**

42-21	A.	Preference in recognition, when no question is pending, is granted first to.	
	Q.	What is the member who has been assigned to make the motion for which a special meeting was called?	*RONR 381*

42-22	A.	Preference status of the member who is presenting a series of motions, when the desired object requires a series of motions, each of which is made following the disposition of the preceding one.	
	Q.	Who is: first while the series is being considered?	*RONR 381*

42-23	A.	Preference in recognition following the adoption of the motion to Suspend the Rules.	
	Q.	What is goes to the person making the suspend motion to present that for which the rules had to be suspended?	*RONR 381*

42-24	A.	When the chair is in doubt as to who is entitled to the floor.	
	Q.	What is decided by plurality vote by the assembly?	*RONR 382*

42-25	A.	The chair makes a mistake and assigns the floor to the wrong person.	
	Q.	What is when a Point of Order can be raised?	*RONR 382*

42-26	A.	Except in a mass meeting, the decision of the chair in assigning the floor can be appealed.	
	Q.	What is may be done by any two members?	*RONR 382*

42-27	A.	If interrupted, action taken by a member who had the floor.	
	Q.	What is takes his seat while the interrupting matter is attended to?	*RONR 384-85*

42-28	A.	The status of a member who, instead of presenting a committee report or other document, hands it to the secretary to be read.	
	Q.	What is does not yield the floor, but has it again when the reading is finished?	*RONR 385*

42-29	A.	Ruling out of order the hollering out of the motion to adjourn, to lay the pending motion on the table, or "Question!"	
	Q.	What is a duty of the chair when maintaining order?	*RONR 385*

Section 43 - Rules Governing Debate

Robert's Rules of Order Newly Revised, 11th Edition - Pages 385-99

43-1	A.	Term that applies to an essential element in making decisions of consequence by intelligent people.
	Q.	What is debate? **RONR 385**
43-2	A.	Term that applies to discussion on the merits of a pending motion.
	Q.	What is debate? **RONR 385**
43-3	A.	The term for the inherent right in a deliberative assembly to discuss the issue.
	Q.	What is debate? **RONR 385**
43-4	A.	The term for the characteristic of all main motions and of certain other motions concerning the assembly's right to discuss them.
	Q.	What is debatable? **RONR 385**
43-5	A.	A right of every member of the assembly that cannot be interfered with except by a two-thirds vote.
	Q.	What is to speak to every debatable motion? **RONR 385-86**
43-6	A.	Amendments or other secondary (subsidiary, privileged, or incidental) motions can be introduced and disposed of.
	Q.	What is action can be taken while debate is in progress? **RONR 386**
43-7	A.	A member may both speak in debate and conclude by offering a secondary motion.
	Q.	What is permitted? **RONR 386**
43-8	A.	A member having been recognized for any legitimate purpose has the floor for all legitimate purposes.
	Q.	What is a parliamentary principle? **RONR 386**
43-9	A.	The phrase the chair may use at the onset and when debate appears to have concluded.
	Q.	What is "Are you ready for the Question?" **RONR 386**
43-10	A.	"Gaveling through" a measure.
	Q.	What is no such thing under legitimate parliamentary procedure? **RONR 387**
43-11	A.	Condition where the right to debate cannot be claimed after voting has commenced.
	Q.	What is when the chair gave ample opportunity for members to claim the floor before he put the question? **RONR 387**

43-12	A.	Action to be taken when voting commences again when debate was resumed after voting on a motion began.
	Q.	What is both the affirmative and negative votes must be called for again? **RONR 387**
43-13	A.	The condition under which debate cannot be resumed except by unanimous consent.
	Q.	What is when a vote is taken a second time for the purposes of verification? **RONR 387**
43-14	A.	No longer than ten minutes unless consent of the assembly has been obtained.
	Q.	What is how long can a member who has obtained the floor speak in debate? **RONR 387**
43-15	A.	Concerning speaking, this can be granted by unanimous consent or by means of adoption of the motion to Extend the Limits of Debate.
	Q.	What is permission to speak longer that the time allow? **RONR 387-88**
43-16	A.	The point at which the chair rises and calls the member's attention by an appropriate signal or by interrupting him.
	Q.	What is when a member's time is exhausted? **RONR 388**
43-17	A.	The point at which the chair can ask for unanimous consent to extend the time for a short period or any member can make the request.
	Q.	What is when it appears the member will need a minute more to conclude his remarks? **RONR 388**
43-18	A.	A member cannot yield any unexpired portion of his time to another member or reserve any portion of his time for a later time.
	Q.	What is rights in regard to debate are not transferable and cannot be reserved? **RONR 388**
43-19	A.	The time used when the speaker yields to another member for a question.
	Q.	What is charged to the speaker? **RONR 388**
43-20	A.	A committee chairman or reporting member is not considered to be debating when presenting or reading the committee's report, but he is bound to obey the assembly's rules relating to debate in any speech made by him in support of the motion offered on behalf of the committee.
	Q.	What is counted as debate when a committee reports? **RONR 388**

43-21	A.	No member can speak more than twice to the same question on the same day.
	Q.	What is a rule of debate? **RONR 388-89**
43-22	A.	The situation where the presiding officer can speak twice (the second time at the close of debate) while remaining in the chair and all other members are limited to one speech.
	Q.	What is debate on the motion Appeal? **RONR 389**
43-23	A.	The asking of a question or making a brief suggestion.
	Q.	What is not counted as debate? **RONR 389**
43-24	A.	The making of a secondary motion so long as in making the motion the member make no comment on the then pending question.
	Q.	What is not counted as debate? **RONR 389**
43-25	A.	Effect on speaking rights if debate on a motion continues to the next meeting held on the same day.
	Q.	What is members who have spoken twice on the motion are not allowed to speak on it again? **RONR 389**
43-26	A.	Effect on speaking rights if debate on a motion continues to the next meeting held on a later day.
	Q.	What is all rights to debate are renewed? **RONR 389**
43-27	A.	The circumstance required before a member can make a second speech on the same motion.
	Q.	What is only after every member who desires to speak on the motion has had an opportunity to do so once? **RONR 389**
43-28	A.	When debate is closed before a member has had an opportunity to make a second speech.
	Q.	What is no second speech can be made? **RONR 390**
43-29	A.	The general rules limiting the length and number of speeches in debate.
	Q.	What is can be modified? **RONR 390**
43-30	A.	The vote required to modify the general rules limiting the length and number of speeches in debate.
	Q.	What is two-thirds? **RONR 390**
43-31	A.	The vote required to change the limits of debate for a session of an assembly.
	Q.	What is two-thirds? **RONR 390**

43-32 A.	The vote to adopt a Standing Rule of the Convention modifying the rules of debate.	
Q.	What is requires a two-thirds vote?	**RONR 390**
43-33 A.	The motion that, whether or not a debatable motion is pending, will change the allowed number of speeches, the length a member may speak, and close debate at a specified future time.	
Q.	What is Limit or Extend Limits of Debate?	**RONR 390**
43-34 A.	The motion that closes debate immediately.	
Q.	What is Previous Question?	**RONR 390-91**
43-35 A.	The motion that prevents any discussion of a subject.	
Q.	What is Object to the Consideration of the Question?	**RONR 391**
43-36 A.	The method that an assembly, by a majority vote, can use to remove restrictions on the total number of times a member can speak.	
Q.	What is go into a committee of the whole, a quasi committee of the whole, or consider the question informally?	
Q.	What is undebatable when applied to an undebatable motion?	**RONR 399**
43-37 A.	Speeches made while the assembly is in a committee of the whole, a quasi committee of the whole, or considering the question informally.	
Q.	What is not counted against a member's right to debate the same question on the same day under the regular rules?	**RONR 391**
43-38 A.	Rules of debate when a document is considered seriatim.	
Q.	What is each member can speak twice on each paragraph, section, or unit when it is taken up as a separate part?	**RONR 391**
43-39 A.	Confining remarks to the merits of the pending question and must be germane.	
Q.	What is a rule of decorum in debate?	**RONR 392**
43-40 A.	Refrain from attacking a member's motives.	
Q.	What is a rule of decorum in debate?	**RONR 392**
43-41 A.	A member can condemn the nature or likely consequences of the proposed motion but must avoid personalities and cannot attack or question the motives of another member.	
Q.	What is the motion, not the maker of the motion, is the subject of debate?	**RONR 392**
43-42 A.	Addressing all remarks through the chair.	
Q.	What is a rule of decorum in debate?	**RONR 392**

43-43	A.	The person speaking can permit an interruption or not as he chooses, but the time taken is charged to him.
	Q.	What is when another member wishes to ask a question of the person who is speaking? **RONR 392**

43-44	A.	Avoid using the names of members.
	Q.	What is a rule of decorum in debate? **RONR 393**

43-45	A.	"The member who spoke last," "the delegate from ...," "the treasurer (or title of another officer)."
	Q.	What is how other members are referred to when speaking in debate? **RONR 393**

43-46	A.	When a member is referring to oneself in debate.
	Q.	What is the use of the first person ("I") is acceptable? RONR 393

43-47	A.	Refrain from speaking adversely on prior action not pending.
	Q.	What is a rule of decorum in debate? **RONR 393**

43-48	A.	A member speaking adversely on prior action not pending should add at the end of his remarks.
	Q.	What is the making or giving notice of the motion to Reconsider or Rescind? **RONR 393**

43-49	A.	A member must refrain from speaking against a motion he made, however, he can vote against it.
	Q.	What is a rule of decorum in debate? **RONR 393**

43-50	A.	During debate, when the maker of a motion changes his mind.
	Q.	What is request permission to withdraw the motion? **RONR 393**

43-51	A.	During debate, a member must secure permission by the adoption of a motion (or unanimous consent) prior to reading from reports and other documents.
	Q.	What is a rule of decorum in debate? **RONR 393**

43-52	A.	Being seated (or if standing at a microphone, step back slightly) during an interruption by the chair.
	Q.	What is a rule of decorum in debate? **RONR 394**

43-53	A.	Action the presiding officer must take if he wishes to participate in debate.
	Q.	What is relinquish the chair? **RONR 394-95**

43-54	A.	When the presiding officer relinquishes the chair, it is first to this person.
	Q.	What is to the vice-president, or to the ranking vice-president who has not spoken and does not decline on the grounds he wishes to speak? **RONR 395**
43-55	A.	Should NOT return to the chair until the pending main question has been disposed of.
	Q.	What is the presiding officer who relinquished the chair and has shown himself to be partisan as far as that issue is concerned? **RONR 395**
43-56	A.	Permitted in small assemblies when a subject is not strongly contested, and should not last more than a few moments, to arrive at a motion consisting of a member's ideas.
	Q.	What is informal consultation to assist the framing of a motion? **RONR 395-96**
43-57	A.	A member may speak when no question is pending on a subject and conclude with offering a motion on that subject.
	Q.	What is allowed in small assemblies if no one objects? **RONR 396**
43-58	A.	Allowed when an undebatable motion is pending.
	Q.	What is a few words of factual explanation? **RONR 396**
43-59	A.	First principle governing the debatability of motions.
	Q.	What is all main motions are debatable? **RONR 397**
43-60	A.	With the exception of the two subsidiary motions that have to do with debate, the degree to which each of the subsidiary motions can be debated.
	Q.	What is depends on the extent to which its application would restrict the assembly in dealing with the main motion? **RONR 397**
43-61	A.	The motion which will kill the main motion, is fully debatable, and the main motion is also open to debate.
	Q.	What is Postpone Indefinitely? **RONR 397**
43-62	A.	The motion which is debatable when applied to a debatable main motion or any other debatable motion, but debate is limited to the merits of this motion.
	Q.	What is Amend? **RONR 397**
43-63	A.	The motion which is not debatable when applied to an undebatable motion.
	Q.	What is Amend? **RONR 397**

43-64	A.	Debate on this motion is limited to the wisdom of referring or to the choice of personnel of the committee and to the nature of its instructions.
	Q.	What is Commit or Refer? **RONR 397**
43-65	A.	Debate on this motion is limited to the wisdom of postponement and the choice of time to which the question will be postponed.
	Q.	What is Postpone to a Certain Time (or Definitely)? **RONR 397**
43-66	A.	The object of these motions is to alter the debatability of the pending motion and their purpose would be defeated if they were debated.
	Q.	What is Limit or Extend Limits of Debate and Previous Question? **RONR 397**
43-67	A.	The right of debate is incompatible with high privilege which could allow for the interference of business.
	Q.	What is why debate on privileged motions is not allowed? **RONR 398**
43-68	A.	An Appeal that relates to indecorum, the rules of debate, or the priority of business.
	Q.	What is undebatable because it is assumed that debate would be a hindrance to business? **RONR 398**
43-69	A.	An Appeal that does not relate to indecorum, the rules of debate, or the priority of business.
	Q.	What is fully debatable? **RONR 398**
43-70	A.	Debate status of an incidental motion to create a proviso.
	Q.	What is debatable if the motion to which it applies is debatable? **RONR 398**
43-71	A.	Debate status of the motion Request to Be Excused from a Duty.
	Q,	What is debatable? **RONR 398**
43-72	A.	The rules of debatability which apply to the motion to Reconsider.
	Q.	What is debatable only to the extent that the motion proposed to be reconsidered is debatable and it opens the merits of that question to debate?
	Q.	What is undebatable when applied to an undebatable motion? **RONR 399**

CHAPTER XIII: VOTING

Section 44 - Basic Classification; Order of Precedence of Motions

Robert's Rules of Order Newly Revised, 11th Edition - Pages 400-06

44-1	A.	The basic requirement for approval of an action or choice by a deliberative assembly except when a rule provides otherwise.
	Q.	What is a majority vote? **RONR 400**
44-2	A.	The word majority means.
	Q.	What is more than half? **RONR 400**
44-3	A.	Term meaning more than half of the votes cast by persons legally entitled to vote excluding blanks or abstentions at a regular or properly called meeting at which a quorum is present.
	Q.	What is a majority vote? **RONR 400**
44-4	A.	Required for any vote to be valid.
	Q.	What is a quorum is present? **RONR 401**
44-5	A.	Term meaning at least two thirds of the votes cast by persons legally entitled to vote, excluding blanks or abstentions at a regular or properly called meeting at which a quorum is present.
	Q.	What is a two-thirds vote? **RONR 401**
44-6	A.	Vote required to adopt a motion that suspends or modifies a rule of order previously adopted.
	Q.	What is a two-thirds vote? **RONR 401**
44-7	A.	Vote required to adopt a motion that prevents the introduction of a question for consideration,
	Q.	What is a two-thirds vote? **RONR 401**
44-8	A.	Vote required to adopt a motion that closes, limits, or extends the limits of debate.
	Q.	What is a two-thirds vote? **RONR 401**
44-9	A.	Vote required to adopt a motion that closes nominations or the polls or otherwise limits the freedom of nominating or voting
	Q.	What is a two-thirds vote? **RONR 401**
44-10	A.	Vote required to adopt a motion that takes away membership.
	Q.	What is a two-thirds vote? **RONR 401**

Here is the Answer! What is the Question? Book 5

89

44-11 A.	Methods for determining if a motion has obtained two thirds of the votes cast.	
Q.	What is take a rising vote (in a very small assembly, a vote by show of hands) and, whenever the chair is in doubt of the results, have the vote counted?	*RONR 401-02*
44-12 A.	Care that the chair should take when dealing with an uncounted two-thirds vote.	
Q.	What is ensure there are two-thirds in favor?	*RONR 402*
44-13 A.	Recourse that the losing side when the chair announces that an uncounted two- thirds vote has been obtained.	
Q,	What is none if the winners choose to prevent a count?	*RONR 402*
44-14 A.	For a vote the proportion that must concur, such as three-fourths.	
Q.	What is one of the elements in the definition of a vote?	*RONR 402*
44-15 A.	Set of members in a vote when not specifically specified.	
Q.	What is members present and voting?	*RONR 402*
44-16 A.	Other often used sets of members for voting.	
Q.	What is the number present, the total membership, or some other grouping?	*RONR 402*
44-17 A.	When an abstention has the same effect as a negative vote, thus the members are denied the right to be neutral.	
Q.	What is when set of members is those present?	*RONR 403*
44-18 A.	An alternative to the requirement of previous notice and is required in order to rescind and expunge from the minutes.	
Q.	What is a majority of the entire membership?	*RONR 404*
44-19 A.	What is done when it is desired that the basis for decision be other than the normal majority or a two-thirds vote.	
Q.	What is the desired basis should be precisely defined in the bylaws?	*RONR 404*
44-20 A.	Term for notice of intent to introduce a proposal that must be given at the preceding (in which case the notice can be oral) or in the call of the meeting at which the proposal is brought up.	
Q.	What is previous notice?	*RONR 404*
44-21 A.	Term for the largest number of votes given to any candidate or proposition when three or more choices are possible.	
Q.	What is a plurality vote?	*RONR 404-05*
44-22 A.	Required to elect to office by a plurality vote.	
Q.	What is must be prescribed in the bylaws?	*RONR 405*

| 44-23 | A. | A condition which might support the use of a plurality in the election of officers. | |
| | Q. | What is an election conducted by mail ballots? | *RONR 405* |

44-24	A.	The times when a presiding officer who is a member of the assembly can vote.	
	Q.	What is when the vote is by ballot?	
	Q.	What is when his vote will affect the result?	*RONR 405*

| 44-25 | A. | When a majority vote results in a tie. | |
| | Q. | What is a time when the chair could vote in the affirmative causing the motion to be adopted? | *RONR 405* |

| 44-26 | A. | When the negative is one vote less than the affirmative on a majority vote. | |
| | Q. | What is a time when the chair could vote in the negative causing a tie and the loss of the motion? | *RONR 405* |

| 44-27 | A. | When for a two-thirds vote the affirmative is one less than twice the negative. | |
| | Q. | What is a time when the chair could vote in the affirmative causing the motion to be adopted? | *RONR 406* |

| 44-28 | A. | When for a two-thirds vote there is exactly two-thirds in the affirmative. | |
| | Q. | What is a time when the chair could vote in the negative causing a lack of two- thirds and the loss of the motion? | *RONR 406* |

| 44-29 | A. | Vote once as a member and then again in his capacity as a presiding officer. | |
| | Q. | What is cannot be done by the chair? | *RONR 406* |

| 44-30 | A. | The principal of why a tie vote on an appeal from the decision of the chair even when the chair's vote created the tie, sustains the chair's decision. | |
| | Q. | What is the decision of the chair can only be reversed by a majority vote? | *RONR 406* |

Section 45 – Voting Procedure

Robert's Rules of Order Newly Revised, 11th Edition - Pages 406-29

45-1	A.	The rights of a member who is in arrears in payment of dues but who has not been formally dropped from membership and is not under a disciplinary suspension.
	Q.	What is has all rights of a voting member except as otherwise specified in the bylaws? **RONR 406**
45-2	A.	Fundamental principle of parliamentary law concerning members and their right to vote.
	Q.	What is each member is entitled to one - and only one - vote? **RONR 407**
45-3	A.	Effect of when a member holds more than one position, each entitled to a vote.
	Q.	What is member can cast only one vote? **RONR 407**
45-4	A.	A member wishes to transfer his right to vote to another member.
	Q.	What is not allowed? **RONR 407**
45-5	A.	A member who has an opinion on a question has the duty of expressing it by voting but he cannot be compelled to vote.
	Q.	What is the right of abstention? **RONR 407**
45-6	A.	A member may vote for fewer candidates than those for whom he is entitled to vote.
	Q.	What is partially abstain? **RONR 407**
45-7	A.	A member who has direct personal or pecuniary interest not in common with other members.
	Q.	What is the member should abstain from voting?
	Q.	What is cannot be compelled to abstain? **RONR 407**
45-8	A.	The policy on voting on questions affecting oneself.
	Q.	What is a member can vote for himself for an office or other position?
	Q.	What is a member can vote when other members are included with him in the motion? **RONR 407-08**
45-9	A.	Not permitted once voting has started except when it is a ballot vote.
	Q.	What is an interruption? **RONR 408**
45-10	A.	"Explaining your vote" during voting.
	Q.	What is would be the same as debate and is not allowed? **RONR 408**

45-11 A.	What a member can do up to the time the result is announced or ask permission of the assembly to grant this request which can be given by unanimous consent or by adoption of a motion which is undebatable.	
Q.	What is change one's vote?	**RONR 408**

45-12 A.	Member may raise a point of order regarding the conduct of the vote.	
Q.	What is a method of challenging a vote?	**RONR 408**

45-13 A.	Member can demand a division for a voice vote.	
Q.	What is a method of challenging a vote?	**RONR 408**

45-14 A.	Member can move to retake the vote under another method.	
Q.	What is a method of challenging a vote?	**RONR 408**

45-15 A.	Member may move for a recapitulation of a roll call vote.	
Q.	What is a method of challenging a vote?	**RONR 408**

45-16 A.	Time when a challenge to the vote can be raised.	
Q.	What is immediately after the chair's announcement?	
Q.	What is before any debate or business has intervened?	**RONR 409**

45-17 A.	Final judge of all questions arising that are incidental to the voting or the counting of the votes.	
Q.	What is the assembly?	**RONR 409**

45-18 A.	What the tellers should do in all questions where there is any uncertainty.	
Q.	What is refer to the assembly?	**RONR 409**

45-19 A.	The usual and normal method of voting on a motion.	
Q.	What is by voice (viva voce)?	**RONR 409**

45-20 A.	Used to verify an inconclusive voice vote or when a two-thirds vote is required.	
Q.	What is a rising vote?	**RONR 409**

45-21 A.	An alternate method for a rising vote in very small assemblies, if no member objects.	
Q.	What is show of hands?	**RONR 409**

45-22 A.	An alternative vote on uncontroversial items.	
Q.	What is unanimous consent?	**RONR 410**

45-23 A.	What the chair should do if he is in doubt of a vote or show of hands vote.	
Q.	What is retake vote as a rising vote?	**RONR 410**

45-24	A.	The chair should do this if he is in doubt and if it is necessary to satisfy himself of the result.	
	Q.	What is obtain a count to verify a vote?	**RONR 410**
45-25	A.	Action a member can take if he feels a voice or show of hands vote is inconclusive.	
	Q.	What is call for (demand) a division?	**RONR 410**
46-26	A.	Action that the members can take to have the vote counted.	
	Q.	What is make and second a motion to count the vote?	**RONR 410**
45-27	A.	The vote required on a motion to have the vote counted.	
	Q.	What is a majority vote?	
	Q.	What is in accordance with a special rule of order establishing the required vote to be less than a majority vote?	**RONR 410**
45-28	A.	Method not used for a retaking of a vote.	
	Q.	What is the same method of voting?	**RONR 410**
45-29	A.	The chair has those in the affirmative rise and stand until counted, then has those in the negative rise and stand until counted.	
	Q.	What is the usual method for a counted vote?	**RONR 411**
45-30	A.	Votes can be counted by having members pass between tellers or having them count off by rows and be seated one at a time.	
	Q.	What is methods of counting a vote?	**RONR 411**
45-31	A.	The doors should be closed and no one should be allowed to enter or leave the hall while a count is being taken.	
	Q.	What is required to ensure fairness of a counted vote?	**RONR 411**
45-32	A.	The raising of a brightly colored cardboard card when asked to do so by the chair when voting.	
	Q.	What is A method of voting that may be used if authorized by a special rule of order or a convention standing rule?	**RONR 411-12**
45-33	A.	A slip of paper on which the voter marks his vote.	
	Q.	What is a ballot?	**RONR 412**
45-34	A.	The method of voting when secrecy is desired.	
	Q.	What is voting by ballot?	**RONR 412**
45-35	A.	The method of voting where it is believed that members may be more likely to vote their true sentiments.	
	Q.	What is voting by ballot?	**RONR 412**
45-36	A.	When the bylaws require a vote be taken by ballot.	
	Q.	What is cannot be suspended, even by unanimous consent?	**RONR 412**

45-37	A.	A motion which would require a member to disclose how he voted in a ballot vote.
	Q.	What is out of order? **RONR 413**
45-38	A.	A motion to make unanimous a ballot vote that was not unanimous.
	Q.	What is out of order unless voted on by ballot? **RONR 413**
45-39	A.	Whenever a vote is to be taken by ballot, moving to have one person cast the ballot of the assembly.
	Q.	What is out of order? **RONR 413**
45-40	A.	Distribute, collect, and count the ballots when voting is in the meeting room.
	Q.	What is the duties of the tellers? **RONR 414**
45-41	A.	To ensure accuracy and enable the tellers when unfolding the ballots to detect any error.
	Q.	What is each ballot should be folded in a manner announced in advance or stated on the ballot? **RONR 414**
45-42	A.	Can always vote in the case of a ballot when other members do and if he fails to vote, cannot then vote without the permission of the assembly.
	Q.	What is what can be done by the presiding officer? **RONR 414**
45-43	A.	To verify that no member votes more than once.
	Q.	What is the tellers' responsibility? **RONR 414**
45-44	A.	The method of collecting ballots.
	Q.	What is fixed by rule or custom? **RONR 415**
45-45	A.	"Have all voted who wish to do so?" (pause), "If no one else wishes to vote... (pause), the polls are closed."
	Q.	What is what the chair says to declare the polls closed? **RONR 415**
45-46	A.	The usual place where tellers proceed to count the ballots.
	Q.	What is in a secluded location or in another room if the meeting proceeds? **RONR 415**
45-47	A.	How blank ballots and other ballots that indicate no preference are treated by the tellers.
	Q.	What is ignored? **RONR 415**
45-48	A.	Counted to determine the number of votes cast.
	Q.	What is any ballot that indicates a preference? **RONR 415**
45-49	A,	If the meaning is clear on the ballot, the tellers do this.
	Q.	What is credit the preferred candidate or choice? **RONR 415-16**

45-50	A.	Status of votes which are unintelligible or cast for an unidentifiable or ineligible candidate.	
	Q.	What is treated as illegal votes?	**RONR 416**
45-51	A.	Status of a ballot containing votes for too many candidates.	
	Q.	What is treated as one illegal vote?	**RONR 416**
45-52	A.	Effect or misspelling of a word or other technical errors on a ballot.	
	Q,	What is as long as the meaning is clear, processed as a vote?	**RONR 416**
45-53	A.	Doubtful ballots that would not affect the result.	
	Q.	What is treated as illegal?	**RONR 416**
45-54	A.	Doubtful ballots that could affect the result.	
	Q.	What is reported to the chair who submits them to the assembly for a determination of how they should be recorded?	**RONR 416**
45-55	A.	Two or more filled-out ballots folded together.	
	Q.	What is as one illegal vote?	**RONR 416**
45-56	A.	A blank ballot folded in with one that is properly filled out is recorded.	
	Q.	What is the blank ballot is ignored and the properly filled out one is recorded?	**RONR 416**
45-57	A.	Status of ballots identified as cast by persons not entitled to vote.	
	Q.	What is not included in the count of number of votes cast?	**RONR 416**
45-58	A.	Status of the vote if there is evidence that there are unidentifiable ballots cast by persons not entitled to vote that might affect the results.	
	Q.	What is null and void?	**RONR 416**
45-59	A.	Method of recording votes on a ballot containing several questions or independent offices.	
	Q.	What is each question or office is treated as if it were a separate ballot?	**RONR 416-17**
45-60	A.	Requirement for counting votes cast on a ballot containing several questions or independent offices.	
	Q,	What is number of votes cast is tallied separately for each question or office?	**RONR 417**
45-61	A.	The recording of a ballot containing blank spaces and filled out spaces.	
	Q.	What is the filled spaces are recorded and the blank spaces are ignored?	**RONR 417**

45-62	A.	The chairman of the tellers, standing, addresses the chair, reads the tellers' report, and hands it to the chair without declaring the result.
	Q.	What is how is the tellers' report presented? **RONR 417**

45-63	A.	The number of votes cast, number necessary for election, votes received by persons, and illegal votes (if any).
	Q.	What is the information in the tellers' report on the results of an election? **RONR 417**

45-64	A.	The number of votes cast, number necessary for adoption, votes for and against, and illegal votes (if any).
	Q.	What is the information in the tellers' report on the results of balloting on a motion? **RONR 418**

45-65	A.	Something the reporting teller never does.
	Q.	What is declare the results of the vote? **RONR 418**

45-66	A.	Action to be taken by the chair following the presentation of a tellers' report.
	Q.	What is the report is read again and the result is declared on a motion, or an officer is declared elected? **RONR 418**

45-67	A.	Action taken on the tellers' report to have it become a part of the official records of the organization.
	Q.	What is is entered in full in the minutes? **RONR 418**

45-68	A.	Action taken with used ballots after the completion of an election or balloting on a motion.
	Q.	What is they can be order to be destroyed or to be filed for a certain length of time with the secretary? **RONR 418-19**

45-69	A.	Time that the secretary retains ballots before having them destroyed.
	Q.	What is until a recount no long can be ordered? **RONR 418-19**

45-70	A.	Period of time during which a recount can be ordered.
	Q.	What is the same session through the next regular session if held within a quarterly time interval? **RONR 419**

45-71	A.	Another session which can order a recount of the ballots.
	Q.	What is a special session held before the next regular session and within a quarterly time period? **RONR 419**

45-72	A.	Preparations should be made in consultation with the person in charge of installing the devices so that all adjustments required are provided for.
	Q.	What is a consideration when using machine or electronic voting? **RONR 419**

45-73	A.	Term for taking a vote by yeas and nays.	
	Q.	What is a roll-call vote?	**RONR 420**

45-74	A.	Effect of a roll-call vote.	
	Q.	What is places on the record how each member votes?	**RONR 420**

45-75	A.	This type of voting is usually confined to representative bodies where the proceedings are published and has the opposite effect of a ballot vote.	
	Q.	What is a roll call vote?	**RONR 420**

45-76	A.	This type of voting should not be used in mass meetings or in any assembly whose members are not responsible to a constituency.	
	Q.	What is a roll call vote?	**RONR 420**

45-77	A.	The vote required to order the taking of a vote by roll call.	
	Q.	What is that specified in the organization's rules?	
	Q.	What is a majority?	**RONR 420**

45-78	A.	Taking a roll call vote in a large society with relative small attendance at the meeting.	
	Q.	What is generally dilatory?	**RONR 420**

45-79	A.	A type of roll-call vote where the voter writes "yes" or "no" and signs the ballot.	
	Q.	What is a signed ballot taken by tellers?	**RONR 420**

45-80	A.	The recording of a signed ballot in the minutes.	
	Q.	What is the same as a roll-call vote but the names of all members need not be called?	**RONR 420**

45-81	A.	A type of vote that cannot be ordered in the committee of the whole.	
	Q.	What is a roll-call vote?	**RONR 420**

45-82	A.	How the chair puts a question for a roll-call vote.	
	Q.	What is the chair puts the question and directs the secretary to call the roll?	**RONR 420**

45-83	A.	Order that the names are called by the secretary in a roll-call vote.	
	Q.	What is the roll is called in alphabetical order except the presiding officer's name is called last and only when his vote will affect the result?	**RONR 421**

45-84	A.	Action of the secretary following each member's response in a roll call vote.	
	Q.	What is the secretary repeats each member's name and answer aloud as it is given and notes the answers in separate columns?	**RONR**

45-85	A.	Action for those who responded "pass" during the first calling of the roll for a roll call vote.
	Q.	What is at the conclusion of the call those who failed to answer can be called again or the chair can ask if anyone entered the room after his name was called? **_RONR 421_**
45-86	A.	After the roll has been called for a roll call vote, the secretary's action.
	Q.	What is the secretary gives the final number of those voting on each side and the number answering present to the chair? **_RONR 421-22_**
45-87	A.	How the results of a roll call vote are announced.
	Q.	What is the chair announces these figures and declares the result? **_RONR 421-22_**
45-88	A.	Entered in full in the minutes when a roll call vote is taken.
	Q.	What is the record of how each member voted as well as the total results? **_RONR 422_**
45-89	A.	Action taken when those answering the roll call do not total a sufficient number to constitute a quorum.
	Q.	What is the chair must direct the secretary to enter the names of enough members who are present but not voting to reflect the attendance of a quorum during the vote? **_RONR 422_**
45-90	A.	A meeting where the roll is sometimes called of an entire delegation.
	Q.	What is in large convention? **_RONR 422_**
45-91	A.	A member demands a poll of the delegates within a delegation in which case each delegate's name is called by the secretary and the delegates vote individually.
	Q.	What is done when the chairman's announcement of the delegation's vote is doubted? **_RONR 422_**
45-92	A.	Adjustments that must be made for the use of electronic roll-call voting.
	Q.	What is presumption of technical and mechanical accuracy of the devices used?
	Q.	What is changes of votes after the result has been announced by the chair on the allegation of machine error are not entertained?
	Q.	What is recapitulation (the secretary reading the names of those voting "aye" or "no") is not permitted?
	Q.	What is if a display board is not erected in the hall members of the same delegation will not be able to ascertain how other members of the delegation vote?
	Q.	What is steps must be taken to prevent members from being able to vote more than once by using a neighbor's keypad or a member lending his keypad to a friend so that the friend can vote for him in his absence? **_RONR 423_**

Here is the Answer! What is the Question? Book 5

99

45-93	A.	The right to vote is limited to the members who are actually present at the time the vote is taken in a legal meeting.
	Q.	What is a fundamental principle of parliamentary law? **RONR 423**
45-94	A.	Absentee voting and must be expressly stated in the bylaws.
	Q.	What is voting by postal or electronic mail, facsimile transmission, and proxy voting? **RONR 423**
45-95	A.	Main reason for the prohibition of mixing absentee ballots with those cast at the meeting.
	Q.	What is through debate and possible amendment, the votes may be on somewhat different questions? **RONR 423**
45-96	A	This type of voting should be reserved for important issues such as amendment to bylaws or election of officers on which a full vote of the membership is desirable.
	Q.	What is a vote by mail? **RONR 424**
45-97	A.	The person who furnishes to the chairman of tellers or other official in charge of issuing the ballots a list of the names and mailing addresses of record of all persons legally entitled to vote.
	Q.	What is the secretary who should certify the list is correct as of the date when ballots are to be issued? **RONR 424**
45-98	A.	Sent to each qualified voter, if the vote is to be secret, in addition to an outer envelope, ballot (without a place for a signature), instructions and information about the nominees.
	Q.	What is an inner return envelope with a space for the voter's signature placed on the front? **RONR 424-25**
45-99	A.	The procedure for ensuring that a teller will have no chance of accidentally observing the vote when removing the ballot from the inner envelope.
	Q.	What is the ballot is prefolded a sufficient number of times so that when returned marked, it is refolded in the same manner? **RONR 425**
45-100	A.	Action of tellers when, in a mail ballot, two ballots are sent in by the same voter.
	Q.	What is contact the voter to determine which is the voter's true vote and, if both are, which (the most recent) is to be counted? **RONR 425**
45-101	A.	A method of voting by which on a single ballot when there are more than two possible choices, the second or less-preferred choices can be taken into account if no candidate or proposition attains a majority.
	Q.	What is preferential voting? **RONR 425-26**

45-102A.	A method of voting when the decision is to be made by mail or at other times when it is impractical to take more than one ballot and can be used only if expressly authorized in the bylaws.
Q.	What is preferential voting? **RONR 426**

45-103A.	Voting method which is preferable to an election by plurality.
Q.	What is preferential voting? **RONR 426**

45-104A.	Term for the power of attorney given by one person to another to cast his vote.
Q.	What is a proxy? **RONR 428**

45-105A.	A form of voting not permitted in ordinary deliberative assemblies unless the laws of the state in which the organization is incorporated require it, or the charter or bylaws provide for it.
Q.	What is proxy voting? **RONR 428**

45-106A.	A form of voting which is incompatible with the essential characteristics of a deliberative assembly in which membership is individual, personal, and nontransferable.
Q.	What is proxy voting? **RONR 428-29**

45-107A.	The reason why a motion to take a straw poll to "test the water" is not in order.
Q.	What is the assembly neither adopts nor rejects the measure? **RONR 429**

45-108A.	Action an assembly can take when it wishes to take a vote on a matter without the vote constituting a final decision.
Q.	What is go into a committee of the whole or a quasi committee of the whole? **RONR 429**

CHAPTER XIV: NOMINATIONS AND ELECTIONS

Section 46 – Nominations and Elections

Robert's Rules of Order Newly Revised, 11th Edition - Pages 430-36

46-1	A.	Term for the proposal to fill the blank in an assumed motion "that ___ be elected" to a specified position.
	Q.	What is a nomination? **RONR 430**
46-2	A.	A form of ballot on which provision is made for voting "for" or "against" a candidate or candidates.
	Q.	What is improper? **RONR 430**
46-3	A.	Are not strictly necessary when an election is by ballot or roll call.
	Q.	What are nominations? **RONR 430**
46-4	A.	Method of voting for one who is not nominated.
	Q.	What is a write in vote? **RONR 430-31**
46-5	A.	Possible result when voting without any nominations.
	Q.	What is repeated many times before a candidate achieves the required majority. **RONR 431**
46-6	A.	The six methods of nominations.
	Q.	What are by the chair, from the floor, by a committee, by ballot, by mail, and by petition? **RONR 431**
46-7	A.	When no method of nominating is specified in the bylaws and the assembly has not adopted a rule on nominations, the method that can be used.
	Q.	What is any member can make a motion prescribing the method? **RONR 431**
46-8	A.	A method of nomination that is a common practice in mass meetings and for committee membership as may be provided in the bylaws or by a motion.
	Q.	What is nominations by the chair? **RONR 431**
46-9	A.	The method of nomination where the chair calls for them.
	Q.	What is nominations from the floor? **RONR 431**
46-10	A.	The number of members required to place a name into nomination.
	Q.	What is one? **RONR 432**
46-11	A.	A second to a nomination from the floor.
	Q.	What is not required? **RONR 432**

46-12	A.	Indicated when a second is made to a nomination.
	Q.	What is endorsement? **RONR 432**
46-13	A.	When more than one person is to be elected to an office or position, such as to a board, a requirement before a member is allowed to nominate more than one person for that office.
	Q.	What is every other member wishing to make a nomination has had an opportunity? **RONR 432**
46-14	A.	Language the chair uses when calling for nominations from the floor
	Q.	What is "Nominations are now in order for the office of ...?" **RONR 432**
46-15	A.	Language the chair says following a nomination made for an office to be filled.
	Q.	What is "... is nominated. Are there any further nominations?" **RONR 432**
46-16	A.	The order followed for calling for nominations for the different offices.
	Q.	What is the order in which the officers are listed in the bylaws? **RONR 432-33**
46-17	A.	Form of nominations done by a small group.
	Q.	What is nominations by a committee? **RONR 433**
46-18	A.	The method by which the nominating committee should be selected.
	Q.	What is elected by the organization or by its executive board? **RONR 433**
46-19	A.	A time when it may be feasible for the chair to appoint the nominating committee.
	Q.	What is when organizing a new society? **RONR 433**
46-20	A.	Unless prohibited in the bylaws, action that the nominating committee can take.
	Q.	What is nominate more than one candidate for any office? **RONR 433**
46-21	A.	Usually not sound to require the nominating committee to do since it can easily circumvent such a provision by nominating only one person who has any chance of being elected.
	Q.	What is to nominate more than one candidate for an office? **RONR 433**
46-22	A.	Members of the nominating committee can be nominated for office.
	Q.	What is should not be prohibited since appointment or election to the nominating committee could be used to prevent a member from becoming a nominee? **RONR 433**

46-23	A.	A desirable policy for the nominating committee to follow.
	Q.	What is contact each person whom it wishes to nominate in order to obtain his acceptance of the nomination and his assurance that he will serve if elected? **_RONR 434_**
46-24	A.	A group from within a nominating committee that may propose other nominees for some or all of the offices in the case where nominations from the floor are permitted.
	Q.	What is the minority? **_RONR 435_**
46-25	A.	A committee that is automatically discharged when its report is formally presented to the assembly, however if one of the nominees withdraws before the election, the committee is revived and should meet immediately to agree upon another nomination if there is time.
	Q.	What is the nominating committee? **_RONR 435_**
46-26	A.	Action the chair takes after the nominating committee has presented its report and before voting takes place.
	Q.	What is calls for further nominations from the floor? **_RONR 435_**
46-27	A.	Action taken if some time has elapsed since the presentation of the nominating committee's report and the calling for nominations from the floor is about to begin.
	Q.	What is the complete list of the committee's nominations is read again? **_RONR 435_**
46-28	A.	All nominations from the floor are completed and nominations are closed for each office before voting for any office takes place.
	Q.	What is a procedure for handling nominations and voting? **_RONR 435_**
46-29	A.	When nominations for one office have been completed, votes are cast for that office and result is announced before the chair calls for nominations for the next office.
	Q.	What is a procedure for handling nominations and voting? **_RONR 435_**
46-30	A.	Action by chair when it appears that there are no further nominations for that office.
	Q.	What is declare nominations for that office closed? **_RONR 436_**
46-31	A.	A method from closing nominations other than the chair declaring them closed.
	Q.	What is use the motion to close nominations? **_RONR 436_**
46-32	A.	A method of nominating that provides members with an indication of the sentiments of the voting body.
	Q.	What is a nominating ballot? **_RONR 436_**

46-33	A.	The results indicate the preferences of the membership without electing anyone
	Q.	What is the value of the nominating ballot? **RONR 436**
46-34	A.	Not permitted when a nominating ballot is used unless authorized by the assembly by a majority vote.
	Q.	What are nominations from the floor? **RONR 437**
46-35	A.	A motion to declare the nominating ballot the electing ballot.
	Q.	What is an improper motion, a nominating ballot cannot take the place of the electing ballot in organizations whose bylaws require elections to be held by ballot? **RONR 437**
46-36	A.	Nomination method used in organizations whose membership is widely scattered.
	Q.	What is nominations by mail? **RONR 437-38**
46-37	A.	A petition signed by a required number of members.
	Q.	What is a method of nominating candidates for office? **RONR 438**
46-38	A.	Ballot voting is done after nominations for all the offices have been closed.
	Q.	What is one of two methods for ballot voting? **RONR 439**
46-39	A.	When the polling place is separate from the meeting room, say at a convention.
	Q.	What is voting for all offices is done on the same ballot? **RONR 439**
46-40	A.	Place in the agenda where the elections should appear.
	Q.	What is early in the meeting in case repeated balloting is required? **RONR 439**
46-41	A.	Votes can be cast for any person who is eligible for election, even if he has not been nominated.
	Q.	What is acceptable in a ballot vote? **RONR 439**
46-42	A.	How results are handled.
	Q.	What is tellers' report is read and chair reads the report again and declares those elected? **RONR 439**
46-43	A.	Action the chair takes when no candidate receives a majority.
	Q.	What is announces "no election" and directs the tellers to distribute new ballots? **RONR 439-40**
46-44	A.	If a candidate receives a majority vote in more than one office..
	Q.	What is cannot hold both unless there is a provision in the bylaws? **RONR 440**

46-45	A.	When a person is elected to two or more offices and is present.
	Q.	What is he chooses which office he will accept? **RONR 440**
46-46	A.	When a person is elected to two or more offices and is absent.
	Q.	What is the assembly should decide by vote the office to be assigned? **RONR 440**
46-47	A.	A ballot vote is taken for each office separately.
	Q.	What is the second method for a ballot vote? **RONR 440**
46-48	A.	An advantage to holding the election for each office on separate ballots.
	Q.	What is the members can take into account who was elected to the previous offices? **RONR 440**
46-49	A.	Action when no candidate receives a majority vote.
	Q.	What is another ballot vote is taken? **RONR 441**
46-50	A.	Is never removed from the next ballot, when the balloting must be repeated, unless the bylaws require removal or he withdraws.
	Q.	What is the nominee receiving the lowest number of votes? **RONR 441**
46-51	A.	Every ballot with a vote for one or more candidates for a board or committee is counted as one vote and a candidate must receive a majority of the total to be elected.
	Q.	What is the method for counting votes when electing multiple positions on the same ballot? **RONR 441**
46-52	A.	An election of members of a board or committee is resolved in this manner when more than the prescribed number receive a majority vote.
	Q.	What is the places are filled by the proper number receiving the largest number of votes? **RONR 441**
46-53	A.	An election of members of a board or committee is resolved in this manner when less than the proper number receive a majority vote.
	Q.	What is all candidates receiving less than a majority vote remain on the ballot for the necessary repeated balloting? **RONR 441**
46-54	A.	All candidates not receiving a majority, including those who received a majority but are tied for the lowest position.
	Q.	What is remain on the next ballot? **RONR 441**
46-55	A.	Necessary action when two candidates tie for an office requiring a majority vote to elect.
	Q.	What is balloting is repeated? **RONR 441**

46-56	A.	The procedure followed when the bylaws require the election to be by ballot and there is only one nominee for an office.
	Q.	What is the election must be by ballot unless the bylaws provide for an exception? **RONR 441**
46-57	A.	The situation where members have the right to cast "write-in" votes for eligible persons.
	Q.	What is when the election is held by ballot? **RONR 441-42**
46-58	A.	A method of election which is applicable principally in mass meetings or in cases where the candidate is unopposed or the election is not strongly contested and the bylaws do not require the election to be by ballot.
	Q.	What is viva voce election? **RONR 442**
46-59	A.	The order in which candidates are voted on in an election by viva voce, rising vote, or a show of hands.
	Q.	What is in the order in which they were nominated? **RONR 442**
46-60	A.	Required action to be taken as soon as one (or as many persons as are required) of the nominees receives a majority vote in a viva voce election.
	Q.	What is no votes are taken on the remaining nominees for that office? **RONR 442**
46-61	A.	When the election is by voice vote and more than one person is required to fill an office, the reason why members wishing to vote for a later nominee should vote against an earlier one.
	Q.	What is as soon as the necessary number have received a majority the voting procedure ceases? **RONR 443**
46-62	A.	Action to be taken by the chair when there is only one nominee and the bylaws do not require election by ballot.
	Q.	What is declare that the nominee is elected, thus effecting the election by unanimous consent or acclamation? **RONR 443**
46-63	A.	The assembly makes valid a viva voce election that the bylaws require to be by ballot.
	Q.	What is something that cannot be done? **RONR 443**
46-64	A.	A method of voting by voice and the member (or chairman of a delegation) declares his vote or votes of the members of his delegation for each office to be filled.
	Q.	What is a roll call election? **RONR 443**

46-65	A.	A method of voting where a member may cast all the votes to which he is entitled for one candidate or divide these votes between several candidates.
	Q.	What is cumulative voting? **RONR 443**
46-66	A.	A method of voting where a minority group, by coordinating its efforts, can secure the election of a candidate of their choice.
	Q.	What is cumulative voting? **RONR 443-44**
46-67	A.	A method of voting that violates a fundamental principal of parliamentary law.
	Q.	What is cumulative voting? **RONR 444**
46-68	A.	Best action to be taken when the assembly wishes to adjourn when an election is incomplete.
	Q.	What is provide for an adjourned meeting to complete the election? **RONR 444**
46-69	A.	Time the election is effective if the candidate is present and does not decline or if the candidate is absent but has consented to his candidacy.
	Q.	What is the election is final immediately? **RONR 444**
46-70	A.	Time the election is effective if the candidate is absent but has consented to his candidacy.
	Q.	What is the election is final immediately? **RONR 444**
46-71	A.	Time the election is effective when the candidate is absent and has not consented to his candidacy.
	Q.	What is when he is notified of his election, provided that he does not decline? **RONR 444**
46-72	A.	Action required when the candidate is absent, has not consented to his candidacy, and declines the election.
	Q.	What is the election is incomplete and another vote can be taken immediately or at the next meeting without further notice? **RONR 444**
46-73	A.	Action which cannot be taken after an election has become final.
	Q.	What is it is too late to reconsider the vote on the election? **RONR 444**
46-74	A.	Unless the bylaws or other rules specify a later time, an officer-elect assumes the position.
	Q.	What is takes possession of his office immediately when his election becomes final? **RONR 444**

46-75	A.	The effect of a failure to hold a formal installation ceremony when prescribed.
	Q.	What is does not affect the time at which the new officers assume office? **RONR 444**
46-76	A.	It is possible for the voting body to order a recount if an election was conducted by ballot.
	Q.	What is in some circumstances? **RONR 445**
46-77	A.	It possible for the voting body to order a recapitulation on a roll-call vote.
	Q.	What is in some circumstances? **RONR 445**
46-78	A.	Normal method to dispute an election.
	Q.	What is a timely point of order? **RONR 445**
46-79	A.	Reason for raising a point of order if an individual does not meet the qualifications for the post established in the bylaws.
	Q.	What is tantamount to adoption of a main motion that conflicts with the bylaws? **RONR 445**
46-80	A.	Reason for raising a point of order when there was a previously valid election for the same term.
	Q.	What is adoption of a main motion conflicting with one still in force? **RONR 445**
46-81	A.	Reason for raising a point of order when a vacancy was filled without proper pervious notice.
	Q.	What is a violation of the rule protecting the rights of absentees? **RONR 445**
46-82	A.	Group with the authority to judge election disputes.
	Q.	What is the voting body? **RONR 446**
46-83	A.	Action which can be taken when an election dispute is immediately pending before the voting body.
	Q.	What is refer the dispute to a committee or board to which it delegates powers to resolve the dispute? **RONR 446**

CHAPTER XV: OFFICERS; MINUTES AND OFFICERS' RE-PORTS

Section 47 - Officers

Robert's Rules of Order Newly Revised, 11th Edition - Pages 447-68

47-1	A.	The minimum essential officers for the conduct of business.
	Q.	What are a presiding officer and a secretary? **RONR 447**
47-2	A.	Where the required officers, how they shall be elected or appointed, their term of office, any qualifications for holding office, and any duties different from or in addition to those stated in the parliamentary authority should be specified.
	Q.	What is in the bylaws? **RONR 447**
47-3	A.	People available to be elected as a officer of an organization.
	Q.	What is usually members, but can be people outside its membership? **RONR 447**
47-4	A.	While the office carries with it only the rights necessary for executing its duties it does not affect these.
	Q.	What is the officer's rights as a member? **RONR 448**
47-5	A.	An ex officio member of the board with full rights as a board member but not the rights of a member of the organization.
	Q.	What is a nonmember holds an office? **RONR 448**
47-6	A.	An officer who is considered to have served a full term.
	Q.	What is one who has served more than half a term in an office? **RONR 448**
47-7	A.	Begins as soon as the officer is elected, unless the bylaws establish a different time.
	Q.	What is the term of office? **RONR 448**
47-8	A.	Ordinarily the term used for the presiding officer of an assembly.
	Q.	What is president or chairman? **RONR 448**
47-9	A.	The term used to refer to the person in a meeting who is actually presiding at the time.
	Q.	What is the chair? **RONR 448**
47-10	A.	The term used to refer to the presiding officer's station in the hall from which he or she presides.
	Q.	What is the chair? **RONR 448**

| 47-11 | A. | The place where other members may make reports or speak in debate. |
| | Q. | What is another lectern should be provided on the side of the platform? **RONR 448-49** |

| 47-12 | A. | Some of the principal attributes of a presiding officer. |
| | Q. | What is have the ability to preside, be well versed in parliamentary law, be thoroughly familiar with the bylaws and other rules, and possess tact and common sense? **RONR 449** |

| 47-13 | A. | To open the meeting at the appointed time. |
| | Q. | What is a duty of the presiding officer? **RONR 449** |

| 47-14 | A. | To announce in proper sequence business that comes before the assembly |
| | Q. | What is a duty of the presiding officer? **RONR 449** |

| 47-15 | A. | To recognize members who are entitled to the floor |
| | Q. | What is a duty of the presiding officer? **RONR 449** |

| 47-16 | A. | To state and put the vote on all questions that come before the assembly as motions and to announce the result of each vote. |
| | Q. | What is a duty of the presiding officer? **RONR 449-50** |

| 47-17 | A. | To protect the assembly from obviously frivolous or dilatory motions. |
| | Q. | What is a duty of the presiding officer? **RONR 450** |

| 47-18 | A. | To enforce the rules relating to debate, order, and decorum. |
| | Q. | What is a duty of the presiding officer? **RONR 450** |

| 47-19 | A. | To expedite business. |
| | Q. | What is a duty of the presiding officer? **RONR 450** |

| 47-20 | A. | To decide all questions of order. |
| | Q. | What is a duty of the presiding officer? **RONR 450** |

| 47-21 | A. | To respond to inquiries of members relating to parliamentary procedure or factual information. |
| | Q. | What is a duty of the presiding officer? **RONR 450** |

| 47-22 | A. | To sign, when necessary, all acts, orders, and proceedings of the assembly. |
| | Q. | What is a duty of the presiding officer? **RONR 450** |

| 47-23 | A. | To declare the meeting adjourned. |
| | Q. | What is a duty of the presiding officer? **RONR 450** |

47-24	A.	A copy of the bylaws and other rules, a copy of the parliamentary authority, a list of all standing and special committees and their members, and a memorandum of the complete order of business.
	Q.	What is items that the presiding officer should have at hand at meetings? ***RONR 450-51***
47-25	A.	What the chair should do when calling the meeting to order, declaring it adjourned, and while putting a question to vote.
	Q.	What is stand? ***RONR 451***
47-26	A.	What the chair should do while explaining his reasons for a ruling or speaking in debate on an appeal.
	Q.	What is stand? ***RONR 451***
47-27	A.	What the presiding officer should do while a member is speaking in debate.
	Q.	What is be seated or step back slightly? ***RONR 451***
47-28	A.	Set up so that the presiding officer when seated can see the entire hall and all present can see him.
	Q.	What is the way the meeting room should be arranged? ***RONR 451***
47-29	A.	What the presiding officer should do whenever a motion is made that refers only to the presiding officer in a capacity not shared in common with other members or if he wishes to take part in debate.
	Q.	What is turn the chair over to the vice-president or appropriate temporary occupant and not return to it until after the motion is decided? ***RONR 451***
47-30	A.	What the presiding officer should do whenever the motion concerns him as in the election of officers or appointing delegates or a committee.
	Q.	What is remain in the chair? ***RONR 451-52***
47-31	A.	Typical temporary occupants of the chair.
	Q.	What is a vice-president, an appointed chairman pro tem, an elected chairman pro tem? ***RONR 452-53***
47-32	A.	Usual temporary occupant of the chair when the president vacates it or is absent.
	Q.	What is the vice-president or first vice-president? ***RONR 452***
47-33	A.	Person, when there is one, whom the bylaws usually place before the vice-president in order to temporarily occupy the chair.
	Q.	Who is: the president-elect? ***RONR 452***

47-34	A.	Title used when there is a temporary chairman other than a vice-president.
	Q.	What is chairman pro tempore or chairman pro tem? **RONR 452**
47-35	A.	Return of the president, the arrival of a vice-president, or by action of the assembly.
	Q.	What is ends of the appointment or a temporary chairman?**RONR 452**
47-36	A.	In the absence of the president and all the vice-presidents, action the secretary should take to open the meeting.
	Q.	What is call the meeting to order for the assembly to elect a chairman pro tem? **RONR 453**
47-37	A.	Required when the assembly expects to elect a chairman pro tem for more than just the immediate meeting.
	Q.	What is previous notice? **RONR 453**
47-38	A.	The practice of permitting the chairman of a committee to preside over the assembly or put questions to vote during their presentation.
	Q.	What is a practice which violates numerous principles of parliamentary law? **RONR 453**
47-39	A.	Action in certain instances, like when the organization is intensely divides on some issue.
	Q.	What is invite a nonmember to serve as chairman? **RONR 453**
47-40	A.	Method to effect having a nonmember serve as chairman for some or all of a meeting.
	Q.	What is adopt by majority vote without objection by president and vice-president(s)?
	Q.	What is suspend the rules over the objection of the president or a vice-president(s)? **RONR 453-54**
47-41	A.	Type of duties of the president in addition to presiding at meetings.
	Q.	What are administrative duties? **RONR 456**
47-42	A.	Source of the authority of the president.
	Q.	What is as provided by the bylaws? **RONR 456**
47-43	A.	Appoints and is an ex officio member of all committees except the nominating committee and maybe disciplinary committees.
	Q.	What is an administrative duty of the presiding officer that must be prescribed by the bylaws? **RONR 456-57**
47-44	A.	The president's status when he has the same rights as other committee members but is not obligated to attend meetings and is not counted in the number required for a quorum.
	Q.	What is when he is an ex officio member of a committee? **RONR 457**

47-45	A.	The term for a person chosen one entire term in advance of becoming president.
	Q.	What is the president-elect? **RONR 457**

47-46	A.	Situation when the bylaws prescribe the position of president-elect.
	Q.	What is the members never elect the president directly?
	Q.	What is members cannot alter their decision regarding succession? **RONR 457**

47-47	A.	The president-elect shall preside or shall fill the vacancy should the president be absent, or if the office becomes vacant between elections.
	Q.	What is usually provided for in the bylaws? **RONR 457**

47-48	A.	Happens in the case of the resignation or death of the president.
	Q.	What is the vice-president or first vice-president automatically becomes president for the unexpired term? **RONR 457**

47-49	A.	Some provision for filling a vacancy in the office of president-elect.
	Q.	What is something which should be in the bylaws? **RONR 457**

47-50	A.	Office holder who usually serves for the president in his absence.
	Q.	Who is: the vice-president (or first vice-president)? **RONR 457**

47-51	A.	Title used when the vice-president is presiding (unless the president is on the platform).
	Q.	What is Mr. or Madam President? **RONR 458**

47-52	A.	Required to overrule the normal succession of the vice-president (or first vice-president) filling the vacancy in the office of president.
	Q.	What is an express statement in the bylaws addressing the filling of a vacancy in the office of president? **RONR 458**

47-53	A.	Typically happens when there is more than one vice-president and the first vice-president fills the vacancy in the office of president.
	Q.	What is the second vice-president moves up to first vice-president, etc.? **RONR 458**

47-54	A.	Something the society should have even though in many instances the vice-president is the logical nominee for president.
	Q.	What is freedom to elect the most promising candidate? **RONR 458**

47-55	A.	The title for the recording officer of the assembly and custodian of its records except those specifically assigned to others.
	Q.	What is the secretary? **RONR 458**

47-56	A.	To keep a record of all the proceedings of the organization--minutes.
	Q.	What is a duty of the secretary? **RONR 458**

47-57	A.	To keep on file all committee reports.	
	Q.	What is a duty of the secretary?	**RONR 458**
47-58	A.	To keep the organization's official membership roll and to call the roll when it is required.	
	Q.	What is a duty of the secretary?	**RONR 459**
47-59	A.	To make the minutes and records available to members upon request.	
	Q.	What is a duty of the secretary?	**RONR 459**
47-60	A.	To notify officers, committee members, and delegates of their election or appointment.	
	Q.	What is a duty of the secretary?	**RONR 459**
47-61	A.	To furnish delegates with credentials.	
	Q.	What is a duty of the secretary?	**RONR 459**
47-62	A.	To sign all certified copies of acts of the society.	
	Q.	What is a duty of the secretary?	**RONR 459**
47-63	A.	To maintain record books.	
	Q.	What is a duty of the secretary?	**RONR 459**
47-64	A.	To send out a notice of each meeting and conduct general correspondence.	
	Q.	What is a duty of the secretary?	**RONR 459**
47-65	A.	To prepare an order of business prior to each meeting.	
	Q.	What is a duty of the secretary?	**RONR 459**
47-66	A.	In the absence of the president and vice-president, call the meeting to order and preside until a chairman pro tem is elected.	
	Q.	What is a duty of the secretary?	**RONR 459**
47-67	A.	Serves in the absence of the secretary.	
	Q.	What is a secretary pro tem?	**RONR 459**
47-68	A.	Person who reads correspondence of an official nature.	
	Q.	What is the recording secretary?	**RONR 460**
47-69	A.	Action the secretary should take with a report.	
	Q.	What is date the report and record on it what action was taken, and preserve it?	**RONR 460**
47-70	A.	Motion not required by the assembly concerning a report presented.	
	Q.	What is that the report be placed on file?	**RONR 460**

47-71	A.	Has the right to examine minutes of the organization at a reasonable time and place.
	Q.	What is any member? ***RONR 460***
47-72	A.	Records that only members of boards and committees have the right to examine.
	Q.	What is the minutes of board and committee meetings? ***RONR 460***
47-73	A.	Responsibility of the secretary relative to records a committee needs to perform its duties.
	Q.	What is turn them over to the committee? ***RONR 460***
47-74	A.	An office to which the duties of issuing notices and of conducting the general correspondence are frequently assigned.
	Q.	What is a corresponding secretary? ***RONR 460***
47-75	A.	The officer the organization entrusted with the custody of its funds.
	Q.	What is the treasurer? ***RONR 461***
47-76	A.	Disburse funds only when granted the authority by the society or the bylaws, make periodic and annual financial reports, and sometimes collect dues.
	Q.	What is duties of the treasurer? ***RONR 461***
47-77	A.	Make a full financial report annually or as the bylaws may prescribe.
	Q.	What is a duty of the treasurer? ***RONR 461***
47-78	A.	Collection of dues and maintaining records of dues status of each member.
	Q.	What is a duty of the treasurer? ***RONR 461***
47-79	A.	Office sometimes established to assist the treasurer in the dues collection and recording functions.
	Q.	What is the office of financial secretary? ***RONR 461***
47-80	A.	Some other officers that can be provided for in the bylaws.
	Q.	What is directors, historian, librarian, curator, chaplain, sergeant-at-arms, and doorkeeper? ***RONR 461-62***
47-81	A.	An officer who sits as a member of the executive board.
	Q.	What is a director? ***RONR 461-62***
47-82	A.	Prepares a narrative account of the society's activities during the term of office which is approved by the assembly.
	Q.	Who is: the historian? ***RONR 462***

47-83 A.	Has custody over the books and other written matter that belongs to the society.	
Q.	Who is: the librarian?	**RONR 462**

47-84 A.	Serves as custodian of any objects of value belonging to the society.	
Q.	Who is: the curator?	**RONR 462**

47-85 A.	Leads invocations and benedictions to open and close the meetings.	
Q.	Who is: the chaplain?	**RONR 462**

47-86 A.	Assists the presiding officer in preserving order, may handle physical arrangements, and ensuring the furnishings are correct.	
Q.	Who is: the sergeant-at-arms?	**RONR 462**

47-87 A.	Makes sure only members and properly authorized persons are admitted to the meeting room.	
Q.	Who is: the doorkeeper?	**RONR 462-63**

47-88 A.	A complimentary title that may be bestowed on members or non-members that is authorized by the bylaws.	
Q.	What is an honorary office or an honorary membership?	**RONR 463**

47-89 A.	Requirement for these to be an honorary office or honorary membership.	
Q.	What is authorized in the bylaws?	**RONR 463**

47-90 A.	Duration of an honorary title or position.	
Q.	What is perpetual unless rescinded or limited by the bylaws?	**RONR 463**

47-91 A.	Has the right to attend meetings and to speak but not to make motions or vote unless the bylaws provide otherwise.	
Q.	What is an honorary officer or honorary member who is not a member of the organization?	**RONR 463**

47-92 A.	Place where honorary president(s) or honorary vice-president(s) should be seated at a meeting.	
Q.	What is on the platform?	**RONR 463**

47-93 A.	Duties of an honorary officer holder.	
Q.	What is none?	**RONR 463**

47-94 A.	The title of the salaried officer who devotes full time to the position of administrative officer and general manager.	
Q.	Who is: the executive secretary or executive director?	**RONR 464**

47-95 A.	Salaried officer in charge of the central office of the society.	
Q.	Who is: the executive secretary or executive director?	**RONR 464**

47-96 A.	The executive secretary or executive director is responsible to.	
Q.	What is the board and the executive committee?	**RONR 464**

47-97 A.	Responsibility of executive secretary to other staff members.	
Q.	What is hires, fires, and determines salaries?	**RONR 464**

47-98 A.	Where the duties and the selection process for an executive secretary should be placed.	
Q.	What is in the bylaws?	**RONR 464**

47-99 A.	The title of a consultant who advises the president, other officers, committees, and members on matters of parliamentary procedure.	
Q.	What is parliamentarian?	**RONR 465**

47-100 A.	Role of the parliamentarian during a meeting.	
Q.	What is purely an advisory and consultative one?	**RONR 465**

47-101 A.	Time when a small organization needs a parliamentarian.	
Q.	What is when they undertake a general revision of their bylaws?	**RONR 465**

47-102 A.	Time when a large, state, or national organization may need a parliamentarian.	
Q.	What is where the transaction of business is apt to be complex?	**RONR 465**

47-103 A.	Typically the person who appoints the parliamentarian.	
Q,	Who is: the president?	**RONR 465**

47-104 A.	To ensure a well-run meeting, when the parliamentarian's main work should be done.	
Q.	What is outside the meeting?	**RONR 465-66**

47-105 A.	A reason for the president and the parliamentarian should confer before the meeting and during recesses.	
Q.	What is to anticipate any problems?	
Q.	What is to avoid frequent consultations during the meeting?	**RONR 466**

47-106 A.	Duty of the parliamentarian during the meeting.	
Q.	What is give advice to the chair?	
Q.	What is call attention to any error in the proceedings that may affect the substantive rights of any member?	**RONR 466**

47-107 A.	Action the president can take if consultation with the parliamentarian is needed.	
Q.	What is ask the assembly to stand at ease?	**RONR 466**

47-108A.	When should the parliamentarian NOT wait to be asked for advice.	
Q.	What is when he sees a problem developing?	**RONR 466**
47-109A.	Time when the parliamentarian may be called upon to speak to the assembly.	
Q,	What is only on the most involved matters?	**RONR 466**
47-110A.	The place where the parliamentarian should be seated during a meeting.	
Q.	What is next to the chair?	**RONR 466**
47-111A.	Status of the parliamentarian's comments on an issue.	
Q.	What is an opinion?	**RONR 467**
47-112A.	A member whose duties include maintaining impartiality and does not vote except in the case of a ballot vote.	
Q.	What is member parliamentarian?	**RONR 467**
47-113A.	Member parliamentarian's right to vacate his chair to speak on an issue.	
Q.	What is none?	**RONR 467**
47-114A.	The power to appoint or elect persons to any officer carries with it this power.	
Q.	What is to accept their resignation?	
Q.	What is the power to fill a vacancy?	**RONR 467**
47-115A.	Has the power to accept resignations and fill vacancies when given full power and authority between meetings.	
Q.	What is executive board?	**RONR 467**
47-116A.	Required to be provided to the members of the body involved with regard to filling a vacancy.	
Q.	What is notice?	**RONR 468**

Section 48 – Minutes and Reports of Officers

Robert's Rules of Order Newly Revised, 11th Edition - Pages 468-80

48-1	A. Q.	A record of the proceedings of an assembly. What is minutes?	**RONR 468**
48-2	A. Q.	Minutes are mainly a record of this. What is what was done at the meeting?	**RONR 468**
48-3	A. Q.	What should NOT appear in the minutes of a meeting. What is what was said?	**RONR 468**
48-4	A. Q.	The kind of meeting; the name of the assembly; the date, time, and place of the meeting; the fact that the regular chairman and secretary were present or if not who substituted for them; and whether the minutes of the previous meeting were approved. What is the content of the first paragraph of minutes? **RONR 468-69**
48-5	A. Q.	All main motions or motions to bring a main question again before the assembly, unless they were withdrawn. What is part of the body of minutes?	**RONR 469**
48-6	A. Q.	For each main motion, how they were disposed of, with the facts as to whether there was debate or amendment. What is recorded in the minutes?	**RONR 469**
48-7	A. Q.	Wording of the motion to be recorded in the minutes. What is the wording in which each motion was adopted? **RONR 469**
48-8	A. Q.	Recorded in the minutes for a motion temporarily disposed of. What is any amendments and all adhering secondary motions that were then pending? **RONR 469**
48-9	A. Q.	How are oral committee reports recorded in the minutes. What is the complete substance?	**RONR 470**
48-10	A. Q.	Appear in the minutes relative to notices. What is record of all notices of motions?	**RONR 470**
48-11	A. Q.	All points of order and appeals together with the reasons given by the chair for the ruling. What is recorded in the minutes?	**RONR 470**
48-12	A. Q.	The place where the hour of adjournment is recorded. What is in the last paragraph of minutes?	**RONR 470**

Here is the Answer! What is the Question? Book 5

48-13	A.	Only recorded in the minutes if ordered by the assembly.
	Q.	What is the name of the seconder? **RONR 470**
48-14	A.	Results of a roll-call vote appears here.
	Q,	What is in the minutes of the meeting? **RONR 470**
48-15	A.	Action to be taken when those responding to a roll-call vote is less than the quorum.
	Q.	What is enough additional names of those present are listed in minutes? **RONR 470-71**
48-16	A.	A record in the minutes of the proceedings of a committee of the whole or a quasi committee of the whole.
	Q.	What is not recorded in the minutes? **RONR 471**
48-17	A.	The place where information on the fact that the assembly went into the committee of the whole or quasi committee and their report can be found.
	Q.	What is the minutes? **RONR 471**
48-18	A.	Information recorded in minutes when assembly is considering a motion under informal consideration.
	Q.	What is same as under the regular rules? **RONR 471**
48-19	A.	The place where a committee report of great importance is copied in full.
	Q.	What is in the minutes if the assembly orders it? **RONR 471**
48-20	A.	Should be entered in the minutes concerning a guest speaker.
	Q.	What is the name and subject of a guest speaker but no summary of the remarks made? **RONR 471**
48-21	A.	The person or persons who should sign the minutes.
	Q.	What is the secretary, and if the assembly wishes, the president? **RONR 471**
48-22	A.	Words occasionally used and represent an older practice that is not essential in signing minutes.
	Q.	What is Respectfully submitted? **RONR 471**
48-23	A.	Action concerning minutes when there is an adjourned meeting.
	Q.	What is minutes of previous meeting are read and approved?
	Q.	What is minutes of adjourned meeting are read and approved at the next regular meeting? **RONR 473**

48-24	A.	Action concerning minutes when there is a special meeting.
	Q.	What is the special meeting does not approve minutes?
	Q.	What is the minutes of the special meeting are approved at the next regular meeting? **RONR 473-74**

| 48-25 | A. | Meaning of the adoption of the motion that the reading of the minutes be "dispensed with." |
| | Q. | What is that the reading and approval of the minutes are not carried out at the regular time? **RONR 474** |

| 48-26 | A. | Status of minutes before they have been adopted. |
| | Q. | What is they are nothing more than a draft? **RONR 474** |

| 48-27 | A. | Action which can be taken if the draft minutes have been distributed to all members in advance. |
| | Q. | What is generally not read at the meeting? **RONR 474** |

| 48-28 | A. | Something to be recognized when draft minutes are made available to the members. |
| | Q. | What is only the official copy of the minutes contains the corrections, if any? **RONR 474** |

| 48-29 | A. | The method for correcting and approving the minutes in organizations that do not meet as often as quarterly and whose meetings do not last longer than one day, or in which there has been a change in a portion of the membership. |
| | Q. | What is the executive committee or a committee should be appointed and authorized to correct and approve the minutes? **RONR 474-75** |

| 48-30 | A. | The method for correcting and approving minutes of a meeting lasting longer than one day. |
| | Q. | What is reading, correcting, and approving of the minutes at the beginning of each day's business or the executive board or a committee is authorized to do the task? **RONR 475** |

| 48-31 | A. | Information that should be written at the end of the minutes to indicate that they have been approved. |
| | Q. | What is the word "Approved" with the secretary's initials and date? **RONR 475** |

| 48-32 | A. | The motion used to correct approved minutes. |
| | Q. | What is Amend Something Previously Adopted? **RONR 475** |

| 48-33 | A. | Title often used when an organization publishes a complete transcript of the meeting. |
| | Q. | What is a proceedings or transactions? **RONR 475** |

48-34	A.	When the minutes or a complete transcript is to be published, this should be done with all reports.
	Q.	What is printed in full exactly as submitted or with all amendments fully identified? **RONR 476**

48-35	A.	The usual meeting when officers report on their work for the year.
	Q.	What is the annual meeting? **RONR 476**

48-36	A.	Form for a report from an executive officer.
	Q.	What is same as for a committee report? **RONR 476-77**

48-37	A.	Required when a report from an executive officer includes a resolution.
	Q.	What is moved by another member? **RONR 477**

48-38	A.	May consist of a simple verbal statement of the cash balance on hand or this balance less outstanding obligations.
	Q.	What is a treasurer's report? **RONR 477**

48-39	A.	A full financial report is presented.
	Q.	What is a treasurer's annual report? **RONR 477**

48-40	A.	The date on which the treasurer's annual report should be compiled.
	Q.	What is December 31 or the date of the last day of the fiscal year if a different year is stated in the bylaws? **RONR 477**

48-41	A.	Action to be taken on the treasurer's annual report.
	Q.	What is no action of acceptance and the annual report is referred to auditors? **RONR 479**

48-42	A.	Action taken on the report of the auditors
	Q.	What is the assembly adopts? **RONR 479**

48-43	A.	In a large organization with complicated financial reports, the group that can audit the reports of the treasurer.
	Q.	What is independent accountants? **RONR 479**

48-44	A.	The group in a small organization that can audit the reports of the treasurer.
	Q.	What is an auditing committee of two or more members? **RONR 479**

48-45	A.	The purpose of adopting the auditor's report.
	Q.	What is relieving the treasurer of responsibility for the period covered by the report, except in the case of fraud? **RONR 479-80**

48-46	A.	When a report is to become a permanent official document.
	Q.	What is the report should be adopted? **RONR 480**

CHAPTER XVI: BOARDS AND COMMITTEES

Section 49 - Boards

Robert's Rules of Order Newly Revised, 11th Edition - Pages 481-89

49-1	A.	The authority by which a board is constituted.
	Q.	What is the bylaws? **RONR 481**
49-2	A.	The group usually empowered to act for the organization between its regular meetings.
	Q.	What is the board? **RONR 481**
49-3	A.	Executive board, board of directors, board of managers, board of trustees.
	Q.	What is names by which a board is called? **RONR 481-82**
49-4	A.	The document that should specify the number of members of the board and how they are determined, defined the duties and powers, and make provision for meetings.
	Q.	What is the bylaws? **RONR 482**
49-5	A.	The officers and a number of directors, managers, or trustees.
	Q.	What is who are commonly members of the board? **RONR 482**
49-6	A.	Time and way of electing directors.
	Q.	What is same as for officers? **RONR 482**
49-7	A.	A requirement that must exist before officers can act as a board.
	Q.	What is the board is established in the bylaws? **RONR 482**
49-8	A.	Only that delegated in the bylaws or by vote of the society's assembly referring individual matters to it
	Q.	What is authority of the board? **RONR 482**
49-9	A.	Condition when the authority given to a board may be limited.
	Q.	What is when the organization meets quarterly or more frequently? **RONR 483**
49-10	A.	Action the board cannot take in regard with previous action taken by the assembly.
	Q.	What is in conflict? **RONR 483**
49-11	A.	The group that can give instructions to the board which it must carry out.
	Q.	What is the assembly? **RONR 483**

49-12	A.	Exception to assembly being able to instruct the board.
	Q.	What are matters placed by the bylaws exclusively under the control of the board? **RONR 483**
49-13	A.	Actions the assembly can take relative to the actions of the board.
	Q.	What is instruct, rescind, or amend if not exclusive to the board? **RONR 483**
49-14	A.	Usually have boards with total authority.
	Q.	What are business corporations? **RONR 483**
49-15	A.	Term for persons on the board by virtue of an office or committee chairmanship held in the organization.
	Q.	What is ex officio members? **RONR 483**
49-16	A.	The ex officio member of the board who is under the authority of the society and where there is no distinction between him and other board members.
	Q.	What is a member, officer, or employee? **RONR 483**
49-17	A.	Ex officio member of the board who is not under the authority of the society.
	Q.	What is a nonmember and non-employee of the society? **RONR 483**
49-18	A.	Has all the privileges of board membership, including the right to make motions and vote but none of the obligations and is not counted in determining if a quorum is present.
	Q.	What is an ex officio member of a board who is not under the authority of the society? **RONR 483-84**
49-19	A.	A board that is not part of an organization.
	Q.	What is board is organized as any deliberative assembly and elects its own officers? **RONR 484**
49-20	A.	Serves as board president in boards which are a part of a society, unless the bylaws specify otherwise.
	Q.	What is the society's president? **RONR 484**
49-21	A.	The group to whom a committee appointed by the board reports.
	Q.	What is to the board? **RONR 485**
49-22	A.	The name of the group composed of a specified number of board members and who has all or much of the power of the board between meetings of the board.
	Q.	What is an executive committee? **RONR 485**
49-23	A.	Term which apply describes the executive committee.
	Q.	What is the board within the board? **RONR 485**

49-24 A.	Rules under which the executive committee operates.	
Q.	What is the same rules as for the board?	**RONR 485**

49-25 A.	If there is one, person who should work closely with the executive committee but be appointed by the assembly or the board.	
Q.	What is the executive secretary?	**RONR 485**

49-26 A.	The document that authorizes an executive committee	
Q.	What is the bylaws?	**RONR 485**

49-27 A.	An organizational action frequently done by a local board.	
Q.	What is organize into committees?	**RONR 485**

49-28 A.	Body the board committees are subordinate to and report to.	
Q.	What is the board?	**RONR 486**

49-29 A.	Not required for a board to establish board committees.	
Q.	What is a provision in the bylaws?	**RONR 486**

49-30 A.	Rules under which the board operates.	
Q.	What is the bylaws, the parliamentary authority, applicable special rules of order or standing rules of the organization, and its own rules (which cannot conflict with the rules of the society)?	**RONR 486**

49-31 A.	Maximum penalty which a board can impose on a person disrupting the meeting.	
Q.	What is he may be required to leave the meeting?	**RONR 486**

49-32 A.	A requirement that must be met by a board which is not a part of a society, when it adopts rules.	
Q.	What is the rules must not conflict with anything in the legal instrument under which the board is constituted?	**RONR 486**

49-33 A.	A meeting of the board where every member has been notified and a quorum is present.	
Q.	What is a regular or properly called meeting of the board?	**RONR 486-87**

49-34 A.	Usual quorum for a board.	
Q.	What is a majority of the total membership of the board?	**RONR 487**

49-35 A.	Status of an approval of a proposed action which is obtained separately by telephone or individual interview.	
Q.	What is not approval of the board?	**RONR 487**

49-36 A.	A requirement that must be met for the holding of a meeting of the board.
Q.	What is members must be present in one room where a matter can be debated and decided as a deliberative body? **RONR 487**

49-37 A.	Requirement to validate decision made by board members not at a valid meeting.
Q.	What is ratification at a properly called board meeting? **RONR 487**

49-38 A.	To whom are the minutes of meetings of the board accessible.
Q.	What is the members of the board? **RONR 487**

49-39 A.	The vote required for the minutes of the board to be produced and read to an organization's assembly.
Q.	What is a two thirds vote, a vote of a majority of the total membership, or a majority vote if previous notice is given? **RONR 487**

49-40 A.	This committee, if there is one, should report at regular meetings of the board.
Q.	What is the executive committee? **RONR 487**

49-41 A.	Groups where members are not required to stand to obtain the floor and can speak while seated.
Q.	What is a small board or a committee? **RONR 487**

49-42 A.	Groups where motions need not be seconded.
Q.	What is a small board or a committee? **RONR 488**

49-43 A.	Groups where informal discussion of a subject is permitted while no motion is pending.
Q.	What is a small board or a committee? **RONR 488**

49-44 A.	Groups where when a proposal is perfectly clear to all present a vote can be taken without a motion being introduced.
Q.	What is a small board or a committee? **RONR 488**

49-45 A.	Groups where the chairman need not rise while putting a motion to a vote.
Q.	What is a small board or a committee? **RONR 488**

49-46 A.	Groups where the chairman can speak in discussion without leaving the chair and in debate, and vote on all motions.
Q.	What is a small board or a committee? **RONR 488**

49-47 A.	The time at which officers are elected, if the board is one that elects its own officers, and committees are appointed.
Q.	What is as soon as the new board members take up their duties? **RONR 489**

Here is the Answer! What is the Question? Book 5

127

Section 50 - Committees

Robert's Rules of Order Newly Revised, 11th Edition - Pages 489-503

50-1	A.	The term for a body of one or more persons delegated to consider, investigate, or take action on certain matters or subjects, or to do all of these things.
	Q.	What is a committee? **RONR 489**
50-2	A.	Unlike a board, what a committee is not considered to be.
	Q.	What is a form of assembly? **RONR 489**
50-3	A.	The term for a relatively small number of persons to give a task detailed attention.
	Q.	What is an ordinary committee? **RONR 489**
50-4	A.	The term for when an assembly designates all of its members present to act as a committee.
	Q.	What is a committee of the whole? **RONR 489**
50-5	A.	That number of times a member may speak in debate in a committee of the whole.
	Q.	What is unlimited? **RONR 489-90**
50-6	A.	The term which includes standing committees and special committee.
	Q.	What is ordinary committees? **RONR 490**
50-7	A.	The term for a committee which has a continuing existence.
	Q.	What is a standing committee? **RONR 490**
50-8	A.	The term for a committee which goes out of existence as soon as its specified task is completed.
	Q.	What is a special committee? **RONR 490**
50-9	A.	A group that, within the area of its assigned responsibilities, has less authority to act independently for the society than a board.
	Q.	What is to whom does the term committee generally imply?**RONR 490**
50-10	A.	Characteristics for holding of meetings of a committee.
	Q.	What is no regular meeting times established by rule but meetings are called? **RONR 490**
50-11	A.	In large state or national organizations, some standing committees function virtually in this manner.
	Q.	What is like a board? **RONR 490**

50-12	A.	When a committee has the authority to take all the steps necessary to carry out its instructions.
	Q.	What is appointed "with power"? **RONR 490**

50-13	A.	Groups that do the preliminary work in the preparation of subjects for consideration.
	Q.	What is the committees for large assemblies? **RONR 490**

50-14	A.	Constituted to perform a continuing function and remain in existence permanently or for the life of the assembly that established it.
	Q.	What is a standing committee? **RONR 490**

50-15	A.	The groups where members serve for a term corresponding to that of the officers.
	Q.	What is standing committees? **RONR 490-91**

50-16	A.	A new group of members is normally appointed at the beginning of each administration.
	Q.	What is standing committee? **RONR 491**

50-17	A.	Methods by which a standing committee is constituted.
	Q.	What is by specific provision in the bylaws?
	Q.	What is by a resolution which is in effect a special rule of order? **RONR 491**

50-18	A.	Needed to permit other standing committees to be created when the bylaws enumerate the standing committees of the organization.
	Q.	What is the bylaws must include a provision that allows for the appointment of additional standing committees? **RONR 491**

50-19	A.	The body to which a standing committee of the organization reports.
	Q.	What is the assembly unless the bylaws provide otherwise?**RONR 491**

50-20	A.	The term given to a committee created to carry out a specified task and on presentation of its final report, it automatically ceases to exist.
	Q.	What is a special committee? **RONR 492**

50-21	A.	Status of a special committee when its assigned task is completed, when it presents it final report to the assembly.
	Q.	What is ceases to exist? **RONR 492**

50-22	A.	Action that may not be done with a task that falls within the assigned function of an existing standing committee.
	Q.	What is assigned to a special committee? **RONR 492**

50-23	A.	Other powers included in the power to appoint members of a committee.
	Q.	What is the power to appoint the chairman?
	Q.	What is the power to fill vacancies? **RONR 492**

50-24	A.	Method of appointment of a committee which cannot be used to appoint nonmembers.
	Q.	What is appointment by the chair without approval of the assembly? **RONR 492-93**

50-25	A.	A method of selection particularly applicable to the choosing of the members of an important standing committee having extensive powers.
	Q.	What is election by ballot? **RONR 493**

50-26	A.	The methods by which the chairman is selected when the committee has been elected by ballot.
	Q.	What is by the committee or the assembly can elect the chairman as a separate position on the ballot? **RONR 493**

50-27	A.	The common method of appointing members to a committee when the assembly wishes to make the selection without voting by ballot.
	Q.	What is nominations from the floor (open nominations) with election by viva voce? **RONR 493**

50-28	A.	The method by which a member is allowed to nominate more than one candidate to a committee at the same time.
	Q.	What is unanimous consent? **RONR 493-94**

50-29	A.	Action the chair can take if no more than the prescribed number of committee members are nominated.
	Q.	What is states that the nominated members shall be the committee? **RONR 494**

50-30	A.	The procedure for electing a committee by voice vote when more than the prescribed number of members are nominated.
	Q.	What is the chair repeats all names in the order in which they were nominated and puts the question on the election of each nominee? **RONR 494**

50-31	A.	The methods the assembly can use to select the chairman of a committee.
	Q.	What is elect a chairman from among the committee members or a chairman can be elected separately, first? **RONR 494**

50-32	A.	The method used to select a committee when the assembly wants to take advantage of the chair's knowledge and judgment but wishes to retain veto power.
	Q.	What is nominations by the chair for committee members? **RONR 494**
50-33	A.	The procedure used when the chair is to nominate the committee members.
	Q.	What is names his choices for members of the committee, always naming the chairman first? **RONR 494**
50-34	A.	Action that can be taken when nominations are made by the chair, after the chair proposes the members for the committee.
	Q.	What is any member can move to strike out one or more names but not insert new ones? **RONR 495**
50-35	A.	The best method and the ordinary procedure in most organizations for choosing members of a committee.
	Q.	What is appointment by the chair? **RONR 495**
50-36	A.	A power that is often given to the president by the bylaws or by action of the assembly in regard to committees.
	Q.	What is the power to appoint members? **RONR 495**
50-37	A.	A power which does not transfer from the president when someone else presides.
	Q.	What is the power to appoint all committees? **RONR 495**
50-38	A.	An exclusion that should be included in the bylaw clause conferring on the president the power of appointment of all committees.
	Q.	What is except the nominating committee?
	Q.	What is except disciplinary committees? **RONR 495**
50-39	A.	The meaning of the phrase "shall appoint all committees."
	Q.	What is the president shall select the persons to serve on committees as the bylaws prescribe or as the assembly may direct to be appointed? **RONR 495**
50-40	A.	A power that is not granted by the phrase "shall appoint all committees."
	Q.	What is that the president alone can decide to appoint, assign a task to a group, and give it the status of a committee? **RONR 495-96**
50-41	A.	The names of the committee members are announced to the assembly, the chairman of the committee being named first.
	Q.	What is required action of the president before a committee can act? **RONR 496**

50-42 A.	Action required when the assembly orders the appointment of a special committee and authorizes the president to make these appointments after adjournment.	
Q.	What is the names of the committee members are announced at the next meeting and recorded in the minutes?	**RONR 496**

50-43 A.	The method used in the case of appointing a special committee when another procedure is not prescribed.	
Q.	What is by adoption of a motion naming members of the committee?	**RONR 496**

50-44 A.	The adoption of a motion naming members of the committee where the names of the proposed members can be included in the motion or added by amendment.	
Q.	What is a method of appointing a committee?	**RONR 496**

50-45 A.	The vote required for removal or replacement of a committee member who is not appointed by the president.	
Q.	What is the same vote as the motion Rescind or Amend Something Previously Adopted?	**RONR 497**

50-46 A.	The president has the power to remove or replace committee members.	
Q.	What is when the power to appoint committees is given to the president?	**RONR 497**

50-47 A.	The body to whom a subcommittee of a committee reports.	
Q.	What is the committee?	**RONR 497**

50-48 A.	The members who can serve on a subcommittee.	
Q.	What is only committee members unless otherwise authorized?	**RONR 497**

50-49 A.	Term for a president who is a member of a committee and has all the rights of a committee member but not the obligation to participate and is not counted in the quorum.	
Q.	What is an ex officio member of a committee?	**RONR 497**

50-50 A.	The resignation of a member of a committee should be directed to this person or body.	
Q.	What is the appointing power?	**RONR 497**

50-51 A.	The person or body that has the responsibility of filling the vacancy on a committee.	
Q.	What is the appointing power?	**RONR 497**

| 50-52 | A. | Characteristics a special committee should have when it is to implement an order of the assembly. |
| | Q. | What is be small and should consist only of those in favor of the action to be carried out? ***RONR 498*** |

| 50-53 | A. | Characteristics of members a special committee should have that is appointed to deliberate or investigate. |
| | Q. | What is persons representing all points of view in the organization? ***RONR 498*** |

| 50-54 | A. | The officer who should provide the committee chairman with copies of papers, the motion or other matter referred to it, and instructions the assembly has given. |
| | Q. | What is the secretary? ***RONR 498-99*** |

| 50-55 | A. | Preserving the papers referred to it and, after its assignment is completed, returning them in the same condition as received. |
| | Q. | What is responsibility of the committee? ***RONR 499*** |

| 50-56 | A. | Action that can be done by the chairman or any two members of the committee unless the assembly rules require a larger number. |
| | Q. | What is call a meeting of a committee? ***RONR 499*** |

| 50-57 | A. | The quorum for a committee meeting. |
| | Q. | What is a majority of the members unless the assembly has prescribed a different number? ***RONR 499-500*** |

| 50-58 | A. | Constitute one session of a special committee. |
| | Q. | What is all meetings? ***RONR 500*** |

| 50-59 | A. | In the nature of minutes, kept by the secretary of the committee. |
| | Q. | What is a brief memorandum? ***RONR 500*** |

| 50-60 | A. | The rules of parliamentary procedure that are followed in committees. |
| | Q. | What is the same rules are for small boards except the rules governing the motions to Rescind, to Amend Something Previously Adopted, and to Reconsider are modified? ***RONR 500*** |

| 50-61 | A. | Role of the chairman of a committee. |
| | Q. | What is to actively participate in the discussions and work? ***RONR 500*** |

| 50-62 | A. | Motions which are not allowed in committee meetings. |
| | Q. | What is motions to close or limit debate? ***RONR 500*** |

| 50-63 | A. | The rules that a committee can adopt. |
| | Q. | What is rules authorized by the bylaws or in the instructions given? ***RONR 500-501*** |

50-64 A.	Members of the organization are permitted to appear before this type of committee meeting and present their views.	
Q.	What is a "hearing"?	**RONR 501**

50-65 A.	The time when only committee members have the right to be present.	
Q.	What is during deliberations of a committee?	**RONR 501**

50-66 A.	Disciplinary action that a committee can employ when there is no opportunity to report to the parent body.	
Q.	What is requiring the disorderly member to leave the meeting room during the remainder of the meeting?	**RONR 501**

50-67 A.	Action a committee can take when it intends to reconvene at another time.	
Q.	What is adjourn or adjourn to meet at a later time?	**RONR 501**

50-68 A.	The intent of a committee whose meeting was adjourned and a time for another meeting was not established.	
Q.	What is meet at the call of the chair?	**RONR 501**

50-69 A.	The motion made when a special committee has completed its work.	
Q.	What is "rise"?	**RONR 502**

50-70 A.	The motion made in a committee meeting that is equivalent to the motion to adjourn sine die.	
Q.	What is to "rise"?	**RONR 502**

50-71 A.	The number of times a year that a standing committee is required to report.	
Q.	What is at least once?	**RONR 502**

50-72 A.	The effect of a standing committee's annual report on matters referred to it for consideration and on which the work has not been completed.	
Q.	What is the work continues with the committee with its new members?	**RONR 502**

50-73 A.	Continues to exist until the duty assigned is accomplished, unless discharged sooner.	
Q.	What is a special committee?	**RONR 502**

50-74 A.	Ceases to exist as soon as the assembly receives its final report.	
Q.	What is a special committee?	**RONR 502**

Section 51 - Reports of Boards and Committees

Robert's Rules of Order Newly Revised, 11th Edition - Pages 503-529

51-1	A.	A document that can contain only what is agreed to by a majority vote at a regular meeting of a board or a committee.
	Q.	What is a board or committee report? **RONR 503**
51-2	A.	A report of a committee that has not been able to hold a meeting due to impracticalities.
	Q.	What is a report containing only what has been agreed to by every one of the members? **RONR 503**
51-3	A.	Relating to a single item of business, often brief, reported as appropriate.
	Q.	What is another form of a board or committee report? **RONR** 504
51-4	A.	The place where recommendations should be located in a report.
	Q.	What is grouped at the end of the report? **RONR 504**
51-5	A.	The group best suited to prepare resolutions to carry out the recommendations.
	Q.	What is the board or committee? **RONR 504**
51-6	A.	A report of a committee to which a single subject was referred.
	Q.	What is a formal report confined as much as possible to recommendations including supporting reasons, if desired? **RONR 504-05**
51-7	A.	Person who can include a brief oral explanation of the committee's recommendations with his presentation and has the right to the floor first in debate.
	Q.	What is the reporting member of a committee or board? **RONR 505**
51-8	A.	Person(s) who can explain in greater length during debate the supporting reasons for the committee's recommendations.
	Q.	What is any member of the committee or board? **RONR 505**
51-9	A.	Danger of inclusion of supporting facts or reasoning in a report proposing certain action.
	Q.	What is may work against the taking of that action? **RONR 505**
51-10	A.	A description of the way in which the committee (or other reporting body) undertook its assignment; the facts uncovered or information obtained; the findings or conclusions; and proposed resolutions or recommendations.
	Q.	What is the form for a report devoted to a single subject? **RONR 505**

51-11	A.	The place where resolutions or recommendations placed within the body of a detailed report also appear.
	Q.	What is repeated at the end of a report? **RONR 505-06**
51-12	A.	Person who presents the report of a board or committee to an assembly.
	Q.	What is the reporting member? **RONR 506**
51-13	A.	The person who presents the report of a board whose chairman is also the presiding officer of the assembly.
	Q.	What is the secretary or another member of the board? **RONR 506**
51-14	A.	The person who normally presents the report of a committee unless he does not agree with it or for any other reason does not wish to give it.
	Q.	What is the chairman of the committee? **RONR 506**
51-15	A.	The person who presents the report when the chair does not choose to give it.
	Q.	What is another member of the committee reports for the committee? **R**
51-16	A.	The time when the assembly receives the report.
	Q.	What is when the assembly hears the report presented? **RONR 506**
51-17	A.	The type of report on which no action is taken.
	Q.	What is a report containing only information? **RONR 506**
51-18	A.	The status of a question(s) when the report contains recommendations which relate only to the adoption or rejection of a question(s) referred while pending.
	Q.	What is that question(s) becomes automatically pending again when the report is given? **RONR 507**
51-19	A.	The action required for the implementation of the committee's or board's recommendation(s)
	Q.	What is the reporting board or committee member usually makes a motion at the conclusion of his presentation? **RONR 507**
51-20	A.	Action not required for a motion made on behalf of a board or a committee consisting of more than one member.
	Q.	What is a second? **RONR 507**
51-21	A.	Action required when the reporting member is not a member of the assembly.
	Q.	What is a member of the assembly must make a motion to implement the recommendation(s) which must be seconded by another member? **RONR 507**

51-22	A.	Action the chair can take to expedite business when it is clear that a motion must be introduced.	
	Q.	What is the chair assumes the motion?	**RONR 507**

51-23	A.	The procedure followed by the chair when assuming the motion.	
	Q.	What is the chair states the question without waiting for a motion to be made?	**RONR 507**

51-24	A.	The effect of adopting an entire report.	
	Q.	What is the assembly endorses every word of a report?	**RONR 507-08**

51-25	A.	The person who can make a motion to adopt the entire report.	
	Q.	What is someone other than the reporting member?	**RONR 508**

51-26	A.	Action that should be taken when the report is to be issued or published in the name of the whole organization.	
	Q.	What is adopt the entire report?	**RONR 508**

51-27	A.	"To adopt," "to accept," and "to agree to."	
	Q.	What is equivalent terms that may be used to adopt a report?	**RONR 508**

51-28	A.	"To adopt."	
	Q.	What is the preferred term for the adoption of a report?	**RONR 508**

51-29	A.	An error often made when the actual intent is to receive the report	
	Q.	What is a motion that a report "be accepted" is made either before or after it has been read?	**RONR 508**

51-30	A.	The effect when the motion "to accept" is adopted.	
	Q.	What is the assembly has endorsed the complete report?	**RONR 508**

51-31	A.	Motions made, or assumed by the chair, to adopt recommendation(s) or resolutions from a report.	
	Q.	What is treated as any other motion?	**RONR 509**

51-32	A.	Action that can be taken on a motion that was referred to a committee who recommends the motion be amended, definitely postponed, or indefinitely postponed.	
	Q.	What is is debatable and (for primary amendment or definite postponement) amendable, under the regular rules for these motions?	**RONR 509**

51-33	A.	A motion that is not in order on a report when the subject was referred to a committee or board.	
	Q.	What is Objection to the Consideration of a Question?	**RONR 509**

| 51-34 | A. | Information that should be shown in an amended adopted report that is published. |
| | Q. | What is the reported version and the changes that the assembly has made? **RONR 509-10** |

| 51-35 | A. | The time the executive board (or board of directors) reports to the assembly upon work done during the year. |
| | Q. | What is annually or at such other times as may be required? **RONR 510** |

| 51-36 | A. | Usually drafted by the president or the secretary, then considered and adopted by the board at one of its meetings before being presented to the assembly. |
| | Q. | What is process for a report of the board? **RONR 510** |

| 51-37 | A. | Person(s) who signs the board report. |
| | Q. | What is signed only by the president or chairman of the board and thesecretary? **RONR 510** |

| 51-38 | A. | The person who moves the adoption of the recommendations of the board (which are grouped together at the end of the report). |
| | Q. | What is the reporting member? **RONR 510** |

| 51-39 | A. | The organization does not need to endorse, can decline to allow to be printed, can adopt only a part, but when printed or recorded must show any changes clearly marked. |
| | Q. | What is options the assembly has concerning a report of the board? **RONR 511** |

| 51-40 | A. | The general form for presenting a committee report. |
| | Q. | What is submitted in writing? **RONR 511** |

| 51-41 | A. | The method of presentation allowed for a report brief enough that the secretary can record its complete substance in the minutes. |
| | Q. | What is an oral report? **RONR 511** |

| 51-42 | A. | The body to whom it is understood that a committee report is addressed. |
| | Q. | What is the assembly? **RONR 511** |

| 5143 | A. | The date of a report. |
| | Q. | What is the date on which the report is presented to the assembly as recorded in the minutes? **RONR 511** |

| 51-44 | A. | How a committee report should be worded. |
| | Q. | What is in the third person? **RONR 511** |

51-45 A.	"The report of the Finance Committee" or "the report of the committee to which was referred ...."	
Q.	What is method of reference to a committee report?	**RONR 511**
51-46 A.	How a report of considerable importance should be signed.	
Q.	What is signed by all members agreeing with the content of the report?	**RONR 512**
51-47 A.	Added following the signature when only the chairman of the committee signs the report.	
Q.	What is the word "chairman"?	**RONR 512**
51-48 A.	The place where it is customary for the chairman to sign when all concurring members sign a report.	
Q.	What is first?	**RONR 512**
51-49 A.	Respectfully submitted preceding the signature.	
Q.	What is not necessary and no longer customary?	**RONR 512**
51-50 A.	Order that reports from standing committees are presented.	
Q.	What is the order in which standing committees are listed in the bylaws?	**RONR 513**
51-51 A.	Order that reports from special committees are presented.	
Q.	What is the order in which special committees were appointed?	**RONR 513**
51-52 A.	Action taken by a committee chairman or other reporting member when no provision is provided in the order of business for reports of committees.	
Q.	What is obtain the floor when no business is pending and inform the assembly that the committee has a report?	**RONR 513**
51-53 A.	The procedure if someone objects to the presentation of a committee report not provided for in the order of business or if the chair is in doubt.	
Q.	What is the chair puts the question to the assembly, "Shall the report be received now?"	**RONR 513**
51-54 A.	Action that should be taken if the vote is in the negative on receiving a report of a committee not provided for in the order of business.	
Q.	What is a later time for the reception of the report should be set either by unanimous consent or on the adoption of a motion establishing the time?	**RONR 513**

51-55	A.	When a standing committee wishes on its own initiative to recommend action on a matter within the committee's concern.
	Q.	What is written recommendations or resolutions at the end of the report? **RONR 514**
51-56	A.	Action taken by the reporting member of a committee on recommendations or resolutions from the committee.
	Q.	What is moves their adoption? **RONR 514**
51-57	A.	Action that any member can take when the committee has offered no motions to implement its recommendations and the drafting of these motions covering them will require further attention of a committee.
	Q.	What is move to refer the recommendations to the same committee or to another committee to draft motions? **RONR 515**
51-58	A.	An item that a report of the committee may contain when a subject on which no resolution or motion was pending has been referred to it.
	Q.	What is conclude with one or more recommendations or resolutions unless the committee recommends no action be taken? **RONR 515-16**
51-59	A.	Possible recommendations that may be made by a committee on a resolution or main motion which was referred to it.
	Q.	What is adoption, rejection, or making no recommendation? **RONR 516**
51-60	A.	Status of the resolution when the committee to which it was referred, reports.
	Q.	What is becomes pending automatically? **RONR 517**
51-61	A.	When stating the resolution, the chair adds "the recommendation of the committee to the contrary notwithstanding."
	Q.	What is when the committee recommends rejection? **RONR 518**
51-62	A.	The content of a report on a resolution or main motion with a pending amendment that was referred to a committee.
	Q.	What is first states the committee's recommendation to the disposition of the amendment and then to the disposition of the resolution or main motion? **RONR 518**
51-63	A.	The contents of a report on a resolution or main motion with a pending primary amendment and secondary amendment which were referred to a committee.
	Q.	What is first states the committee's recommendation to the disposition of the secondary amendment, then the primary amendment, and then the resolution or main motion? **RONR 518-19**

51-64 A.	The method the chair follows for handling the committee's recommendations to the disposition of the secondary amendment, the primary amendment, and the resolution or main motion.
Q.	What is the chair states the question and takes the vote first on the secondary amendment, then on the primary amendment, and finally on the resolution? **RONR 518**
51-65 A.	The consequence of the motion Postpone Indefinitely which is pending when a motion is referred to a committee.
Q.	What is ignored when the committee reports? **RONR 519**
51-66 A.	The time when a reporting member makes the motion to Postpone to a Certain Time when reporting on a pending resolution or main motion that may or may not also include a pending amendment.
Q.	What is at the conclusion of his presentation? **RONR 519**
51-67 A.	The procedure for making the motion Postpone Indefinitely when reporting on a resolution or main motion with a pending amendment reporting.
Q.	What is the member makes the motion Postpone Indefinitely after a pending amendment has been voted on? **RONR 519**
51-68 A.	The method a committee should use when it reports back on a pending resolution and proposed amendments.
Q.	What is unless very simple, in writing, on a separate sheet of paper? **RONR 520**
51-69 A.	Action to be taken by the reporting member when the committee proposes amendments to a pending resolution or main motion or a secondary amendment to a pending primary amendment.
Q.	What is moves the adoption of amendments proposed by the committee at the conclusion of the report? **RONR 521**
51-70 A.	Action to be taken by the reporting member when the committee proposes an additional amendment(s) to a pending resolution or main motion with a pending amendment(s).
Q.	What is makes the proposed additional amendment(s) following the disposal of the pending amendment(s)? **RONR 521-22**
51-71 A.	An alternative where the chair puts a single question on all of the committee's amendments together.
Q.	What is putting the question on the amendments in gross? **RONR 523**
51-72 A.	Action to be taken when a committee proposes to substitute a new motion for a motion referred to it when no amendment was pending.
Q.	What is the reporting member makes the motion to substitute at the conclusion of his presentation? **RONR 524**

51-73	A.	Action to be taken when a committee proposes to substitute a new motion for a motion referred to it with pending amendment(s).
	Q.	What is the reporting member makes the motion to substitute following the vote on the pending amendment(s)? **RONR 524**

51-74	A.	Action on a committee report containing only information.
	Q.	What is none? **RONR 525**

51-75	A.	The membership committee's report can be presented orally, but the list of names of persons recommended for membership should be in this form.
	Q.	What is in writing? **RONR 525**

51-76	A.	Action the chair takes following a membership committee's report on names of persons referred to the committee as applicants for membership.
	Q.	What is states the question on the admission to membership of the persons recommended? **RONR 525**

51-77	A.	Vote on the report of the nominating committee.
	Q.	What is none? **RONR 525**

51-78	A.	Action to be taken when a brief committee report is given orally.
	Q.	What is the complete substance of the report is recorded in the minutes? **RONR 526**

51-79	A.	The method of handling a partial report of a committee.
	Q.	What is the same way as a final report? **RONR 527**

51-80	A.	Vote required to discharge a special committee when it presents a partial report.
	Q.	What is majority vote? **RONR 527**

51-81	A.	The term for a report expressing the views of a group of committee members not agreeing with the committee's report.
	Q.	What is a minority report? **RONR 527**

51-82	A.	Referred to by the term "committee report."
	Q.	What is the report adopted by a majority of the committee members? **RONR 527**

51-83	A.	The formal presentation of a minority report.
	Q.	What is a privilege that the assembly may grant? **RONR 527-28**

51-84	A.	In debate on a report members who do not concur may speak in opposition.
	Q.	What is any member including members of the committee? **RONR 528**

| 51-85 | A. | Conditions under which a reference is allowed to what has occurred during the deliberations of the committee. |
| | Q. | What is only if it is in the report of the committee or by unanimous consent of the members of the committee? **RONR 528** |

| 51-86 | A. | A suggested form for the beginning of a minority report |
| | Q. | What is "The undersigned, a minority of the committee appointed to ..., not agreeing with the majority, desire to express their views in the case ..."? **RONR 528** |

| 51-87 | A. | The content of the minority report when the committee report is only for information. |
| | Q. | What is can be constructed similarly to any report and may conclude with a motion? **RONR 528** |

| 51-88 | A. | A report that is presented immediately following a report of the committee if the assembly grants permission. |
| | Q. | What is a minority report? **RONR 528** |

| 51-89 | A. | The procedure to be taken for the minority report to become the report of the committee. |
| | Q. | What is by the adoption of a motion to substitute the minority report for the committee report? **RONR 529** |

| 51-90 | A. | The person who can make the motion that the resolutions proposed by the committee be amended, be postponed indefinitely, or that some other appropriate action be taken. |
| | Q. | What is any member? **RONR 529** |

| 51-91 | A. | Action that a member who is in agreement with a report except for one part can take when signing the report. |
| | Q. | What is add a statement that he concurs with the report except the part specified and sign that statement? **RONR 529** |

Section 52 - Committee of the Whole and Its Alternate Forms

Robert's Rules of Order Newly Revised, 11th Edition - Pages 529-42

52-1	A.	Devices that enable the full assembly to give detailed consideration to a matter under conditions of freedom similar to those of a committee.
	Q.	What is the committee of the whole, quasi committee of the whole, and informal consideration? **RONR 529**
52-2	A.	The rules of debate for an assembly meeting as a committee of the whole, quasi committee of the whole, or in informal consideration.
	Q.	What is a member can speak in debate on the main motion or any amendment for the same length of time as allowed by assembly rules and as often as he is able to obtain the floor but he cannot speak another time on the same question as long as a member who has not spoken is seeking to speak? **RONR 529-30**
52-3	A.	The device best suited to large assemblies of more than 100 members to allow it to act as if it is a committee.
	Q.	What is a committee of the whole? **RONR 530**
52-4	A.	The status of decisions made in a committee of the whole or a quasi committee of the whole.
	Q.	What is votes have the status of recommendations? **RONR 530**
52-5	A.	Presides in a committee of the whole.
	Q.	What is a chairman is appointed and the regular presiding officer leaves the chair? **RONR 530**
52-6	A.	A reason that in a committee of the whole the regular presiding officer does not remain in the chair.
	Q.	What is he may be in a better position to preside effectively during the final consideration by the assembly? **RONR 530**
52-7	A.	The device best suited to assemblies of medium size (about 50 to 100) to allow it to act as if it is a committee.
	Q.	What is a quasi committee of the whole? **RONR 530**
52-8	A.	Presides in a quasi committee of the whole or when the assembly is in informal consideration.
	Q.	What is the presiding officer remains in the chair and presides? **RONR 530**
52-9	A.	The device best suited to small assemblies of ordinary societies to allow it to act as if it is a committee.
	Q.	What is informal consideration? **RONR 530**

52-10	A.	Effect of going into informal consideration.
	Q.	What is normal limits on number of times a member can speak on any motion in debate are removed? **RONR 530-31**
52-11	A.	The status of decisions made in informal consideration.
	Q.	What is the results of votes are decisions of the assembly and not voted on again? **RONR 530-31**
52-12	A.	The oldest of the three devices and not used extensively except in legislative bodies.
	Q.	What is committee of the whole? **RONR 531**
52-13	A.	When the assembly is meeting in this form, the meeting is technically not "the assembly."
	Q.	What is as a committee of the whole? **RONR 531**
52-14	A.	The parliamentary steps in making use of a committee of the whole.
	Q.	What is essentially the same as those involved in referring a subject to an ordinary committee? **RONR 531**
52-15	A.	The steps for handling a subject referred to a committee of the whole.
	Q.	What is the assembly votes to go into a committee of the whole, a chairman of the committee is appointed, the committee considers the referred matter and adopts a report to be made to the assembly, the committee votes to "rise and report," the committee chairman presents the report to the assembly, and the recommendations are considered? **RONR 531**
52-16	A.	A motion to go into a committee of the whole is a form of this motion.
	Q.	What is Commit? **RONR 531-32**
52-17	A.	The person who frequently presides in a committee of the whole.
	Q.	What is the vice-president? **RONR 532**
52-18	A.	Action taken by the usual presiding officer during deliberations in a committee of the whole.
	Q.	What is the presiding officer takes his place as a member of the committee? **RONR 532**
52-19	A.	The person who keeps a memorandum of the business transacted in a committee of the whole.
	Q.	What is the secretary, if he does not leave his seat, or an assistant secretary or clerk may act as secretary? **RONR 532**

52-20	A.	Information to be recorded in the assembly's minutes concerning a meeting of a committee of the whole.
	Q.	What is the minutes should indicate the referral to a committee of the whole, the committee's report, and the assembly's action on the report? **RONR 532**
52-21	A.	Action that can or cannot be taken in a committee of the whole on a resolution referred to it.
	Q.	What is the committee cannot alter the text of any resolution referred to it; it can propose amendments; originate new resolutions; and reports in the form of recommendations to the assembly? **RONR 532**
52-22	A.	Motions that are in order in committee of the whole.
	Q.	What is to adopt (within the committee for inclusion in the report)?
	Q.	What is to amend what is proposed in the report?
	Q.	What is to "rise and report"?
	Q.	What is incidental motions point of order, appeal from the decision of the chair, division of the assembly, and applicable requests and inquiries? **RONR 533**
52-23	A.	The meaning of the term to rise as applied to a committee in general.
	Q.	What is the parliamentary step of ceasing to function as a committee? **RONR 533n**
52-24	A.	The rule on speaking in debate in a committee of the whole unless a limit is prescribed by the assembly before it goes into committee.
	Q.	What is each member can speak an unlimited number of times? **RONR 533**
52-25	A.	Action that must be taken to adopt a motion not allowed in a committee of the whole.
	Q.	What is the committee must rise and report a recommendation that the assembly take the desired action? **RONR 533**
52-26	A.	Characteristics of the motion to rise and report.
	Q.	What are requires recognition, undebatable, and cannot be amended and always in order in a committee of a whole except during voting or verifying a vote? **RONR 533-34**
52-27	A.	In a committee of the whole, action taken to appoint a subcommittee or refer a matter to another committee.
	Q.	What is not allowed? **RONR 534**
52-28	A.	In a committee of the whole, limitations and requirements for handling an appeal.
	Q.	What is cannot be postponed or laid on the table and must be voted on immediately? **RONR 534**

52-29	A.	Allowed procedures for debate to be closed or limited in a committee of the whole.
	Q.	What is must be specified before going into committee of the whole? *RONR 534*
52-30	A.	Action required if the committee of the whole develops a desire to have debate limited or extended.
	Q.	What is rising and requesting the assembly impose the desired limits? *RONR 534*
52-31	A.	Methods of voting not allowed in a committee of the whole.
	Q.	What is voting by roll call, by ballot, or a counted rising vote (unless ordered by the chair)? *RONR 534*
52-32	A.	Action that can be taken by a committee of the whole when it wishes to impose disciplinary measures on its members.
	Q.	What is report the facts to the assembly? *RONR 534*
52-33	A.	Action that can be taken if the committee becomes disorderly and its chairman loses control.
	Q.	What is the presiding officer of the assembly takes the chair and declares the committee of the whole dissolved? *RONR 534*
52-34	A.	Privileged motions that are out of order when the assembly is meeting as a committee of the whole.
	Q.	What is adjourn or recess? *RONR 534*
52-35	A.	A circumstance under which a committee of the whole concludes its work by voting to report a resolution.
	Q.	What is when the committee originates a resolution? *RONR 535*
52-36	A.	A circumstance under which a committee of the whole concludes its work by voting on amendments that it will recommend.
	Q.	What is when the committee proposes amendments on a resolution referred to it? *RONR 535*
52-37	A.	Procedure for handling recommendations made by the committee of the whole.
	Q.	What is the same rules as for the handling of reports and recommendations made by any other committee? *RONR 535*
52-38	A.	Action taken by a committee of the whole when requesting instructions from the assembly.
	Q.	What is agrees to the wording of the request before adopting the motion to rise? *RONR 536*

Here is the Answer! What is the Question? Book 5

147

52-39	A.	If a committee of the whole wishes to bring its proceedings to an end or wants the meeting to be adjourned.
	Q.	What is it must first rise and report? **RONR 536**
52-40	A.	The time when a committee of the whole passes out of existence unless directed to sit again.
	Q.	What is when the committee has made its report? **RONR 537**
52-41	A.	The granting of the request by a committee of the whole to sit again without specifying a time.
	Q.	What is the sitting is unfinished business? **RONR 537**
52-42	A.	Action taken by a committee of the whole when the hour of adjournment, which has been preset for the assembly, is reached.
	Q.	What is the committee chairman announces the fact and states that "the committee will rise" followed by a report to the assembly that the committee has come to no conclusion on the referred matter? **RONR 537**
52-43	A.	Quorum in a committee of the whole.
	Q.	What is the same as the assembly unless the assembly established a different one prior to going into committee? **RONR 537**
52-44	A.	Action that must be taken if a committee of the whole finds itself without a quorum.
	Q.	What is the committee must rise and report to the assembly which must then adjourn, if it itself is without a quorum, or take one of the other options that are open in the absence of a quorum? **RONR 537-38**
52-45	A.	The committee device that is appropriate for an assembly of medium size acting as if in a committee of the whole.
	Q.	What is a quasi committee of the whole? **RONR 538**
52-46	A.	The person who presides in a quasi committee of the whole.
	Q.	What is the presiding officer of the assembly? **RONR 538**
52-47	A.	The responsibility of the secretary in a quasi committee of the whole.
	Q.	What is keeps a temporary memorandum of the business transacted? **RONR 538-39**
52-48	A.	Recorded in the minutes of the assembly who has met as a quasi committee of the whole.
	Q.	What is only a record of the report and the action taken? **RONR 539**

52-49	A.	Procedures for conducting business in a quasi committee of the whole.
	Q.	What is the same as in a committee of the whole except that any motion that would be in order in the assembly is in order while meeting in committee? **RONR 539**
52-50	A.	The results of the quasi committee of the whole adopting a motion other than a motion to amend.
	Q.	What is automatically puts an end to the proceedings? **RONR 539**
52-51	A.	When a quasi committee of the whole reports, the procedure for taking action on its recommendations.
	Q.	What is the presiding officer immediately proceeds to report to the assembly and to state the question on proposed amendments? **RONR 539-540**
52-52	A.	The method for handling consideration of reported amendment(s) from a quasi committee of the whole.
	Q.	What is the chair puts the question on reported amendments in gross, except for those for which a separate vote has been asked? **RONR 540**
52-53	A.	The rule suspended when an assembly considers a question informally.
	Q.	What is the rule that limits the number of times a member may speak in debate on the main motion and any proposed amendments? **RONR 540**
52-54	A.	What the assembly's minutes reflect for action taken when the assembly is in informal consideration.
	Q.	What is proceedings are recorded? **RONR 541**
52-55	A.	Limits on debate that are allowed when the assembly is considering a motion informally.
	Q.	What is any approved by the assembly? **RONR 541**
52-56	A.	Action taken that automatically closes informal consideration.
	Q.	What is the main motion is disposed of temporarily or permanently? **RONR 541**
52-57	A.	Adoption of a motion by majority vote "that the regular rules of debate be in force," or "that the question be considered formally."
	Q.	What is ends informal consideration? **RONR 541**
52-58	A.	A practice that has developed in recent years where every member in attendance is urged to participate in a group.
	Q.	What is breakout groups? **RONR 541**

CHAPTER XVII: MASS MEETINGS;
ORGANIZATION OF A PERMANENT SOCIETY

Section 53 - Mass Meetings

Robert's Rules of Order Newly Revised, 11th Edition - Pages 543-53

53-1	A.	Name for a meeting of an unorganized group.	
	Q.	What is a mass meeting?	**RONR 543**
53-2	A.	The publicized or selectively distributed notice used to advertise a mass meeting.	
	Q.	What is the call?	**RONR 543**
53-3	A.	Called to take appropriate action on a particular problem or towards a particular purpose.	
	Q.	What is purpose of a mass meeting?	**RONR 543**
53-4	A.	Everyone interested in the stated problem or purpose.	
	Q.	What is to whom the mass meeting is open?	**RONR 543**
53-5	A.	Only these have the right to make motions, to speak, or to vote in a mass meeting.	
	Q.	What is persons in the invited category?	**RONR 543-44**
53-6	A.	Those who have the right to control the overall objective of a mass meeting.	
	Q.	What is the sponsors?	**RONR 544**
53-7	A.	Should specify the date, hour, and place of the meeting, its purpose, who is invited to attend, and may include identification of the sponsorship.	
	Q.	What is information included in the call or announcement for a mass meeting?	**RONR 544**
53-8	A.	Announcements in the newspapers or by radio or television, mailings, posters, handbills or flyers, or the like.	
	Q.	What is methods to advertise the mass meeting?	**RONR 544**
53-9	A.	Done by the sponsors to avoid the risk of the assembly's floundering.	
	Q.	What is a certain amount of planning?	**RONR 544**
53-10	A.	Competent as a presiding officer and in sympathy with the object of the mass meeting.	
	Q.	What are characteristics for the chairman of a mass meeting?	**RONR 545**

| 53-11 | A. | Having a set of resolutions drafted in advance to submit. | |
| | Q. | What is a good policy? | *RONR 545* |

| 53-12 | A. | The name for all the persons in the invited category who attend a mass meeting. | |
| | Q. | What is the membership? | *RONR 545* |

| 53-13 | A. | When no qualification is made in the call to a mass meeting, the rights of any person in attendance. | |
| | Q. | What is the same as the rights of members in an assembly? | *RONR 545* |

| 53-14 | A. | Can be asked to leave a mass meeting. | |
| | Q. | What is a person discovered to have entered fraudulently? | *RONR 545* |

| 53-15 | A. | When there is no mention in the call, the parliamentary authority used at a mass meeting. | |
| | Q. | What is a recognized parliamentary manual? | *RONR 546* |

| 53-16 | A. | Time when the sponsors should have a parliamentary authority adopted. | |
| | Q. | What is immediately after the election of a secretary? | *RONR 546* |

| 53-17 | A. | The force of provisions of the call specifying the mass meeting's purpose and those invited to attend it. | |
| | Q. | What is equivalent to bylaws of an organized society? | *RONR 546* |

| 53-18 | A. | Define the subject matter within which motions or resolutions are in order, and determine who have the right to participate as members. | |
| | Q. | What is provisions in the call for the meeting? | *RONR 546* |

| 53-19 | A. | The first two items in the order of business at a mass meeting. | |
| | Q. | What are election of chairman and election of secretary? | *RONR 547* |

| 53-20 | A. | Usual method of electing chairman and the secretary at a mass meeting. | |
| | Q. | What is voice vote? | *RONR 547* |

| 53-21 | A. | A name chosen by the sponsors is the first nomination for chairman. | |
| | Q. | What is the usual process? | *RONR 547* |

| 53-22 | A. | Person who conducts the election for chairman. | |
| | Q. | Who is: the person calling the meeting to order? | *RONR 547* |

| 53-23 | A. | The first action of the newly elected chairman. | |
| | Q. | What is call for nominations for secretary? | *RONR 547* |

53-24 A.	Item of business immediately following election of the secretary at a mass meeting.	
Q.	What is read the call to the meeting?	**RONR 548**

53-25 A.	Business which follows the reading of the call.	
Q.	What is an explanation of the purpose for the meeting?	**RONR 548**

53-26 A.	In order after the purpose for which the mass meeting was called has been explained.	
Q.	What is a member offers resolution(s) to accomplish purpose?	**RONR 548**

53-27 A.	Any motion within the scope of the meeting's purpose as announced in the call.	
Q.	What is in order?	**RONR 549**

53-28 A.	Any motion contrary to the purpose of the meeting as announced in the call.	
Q.	What is out of order?	**RONR 549**

53-29 A.	Not allowed relative to the assigning of the floor in a mass meeting.	
Q.	What is appeal from the chair's decision?	**RONR 549**

53-30 A.	A committee should be appointed at the meeting to draft resolutions.	
Q.	What is if resolutions are not prepared in advance?	**RONR 549**

53-31 A.	Those present can make brief statements after the initial explanation of the meeting's purpose and before the motion to appoint a committee.	
Q.	What is can be permitted by the chairman?	**RONR 549**

53-32 A.	Permitted in a mass meeting but generally not allowed in a meeting of an ordinary society.	
Q.	What is informal discussion with no motion on the floor?	**RONR 549**

53-33 A.	Person to make the motion to appoint a committee.	
Q.	What is should be agreed upon before the meeting?	**RONR 550**

53-34 A.	Advisable method of appointment of committees at a mass meeting.	
Q.	What is by the chair?	**RONR 550**

53-35 A.	Immediately retire and prepare the resolution(s).	
Q.	What is what the committee should do once appointed?	**RONR 550**

53-36 A.	Chairman of the committee reports the results and then does this.	
Q.	What is moves the proposed resolution?	**RONR 551**

53-37	A.	Status of the committee following the making of the motion concerning the proposed resolution.
	Q.	What is discharged? **RONR 551**

53-38	A.	In a mass meeting, this motion is not in order while business is pending.
	Q.	What is the motion to Adjourn? **RONR 551**

53-39	A.	What usually happens with the adoption of the motion to Adjourn at a mass meeting.
	Q.	What is dissolves the assembly? **RONR 552**

53-40	A.	Status of the motion to Adjourn when business has not been completed and the time for another meeting has already been set.
	Q.	What is it is a privileged motion? **RONR 552**

53-41	A.	When business has not been completed, the recommended action before adoption of the motion to Adjourn.
	Q.	What is fix the time for an adjourned meeting? **RONR 552**

53-42	A.	Action upon adoption of the motion to Adjourn when no further meeting has been set.
	Q.	What is the assembly is dissolved? **RONR 552**

53-43	A.	Title of officers when mass meeting forms a temporary organization.
	Q.	What is chairman pro tem and secretary pro tem? **RONR 553**

53-44	A.	Term of temporary officers.
	Q.	What is until permanent officers are elected? **RONR 553**

53-45	A.	When rules are adopted which specify periodic dates on which meetings are to be held, status of these meetings.
	Q.	What is each individual meeting is a session? **RONR 553**

53-46	A.	Session structure when there is need for a series of meetings of a temporary organization and each meeting is set at the previous meeting.
	Q.	What is the entire series of meetings constitutes a single session? **RONR 553**

Robert's Rules of Order Newly Revised, 11th Edition - Pages 553-61

54-1	A.	The first meeting to form a permanent organization is conducted like this.
	Q.	What is a mass meeting? **RONR 553**
54-2	A.	Attendance at the first meeting to organize a permanent organization should be carefully limited to these.
	Q.	What is persons whose interest in the project is known? **RONR 553-54**
54-3	A.	The first item of business at a meeting to organize a permanent organization.
	Q.	What is elect a chairman pro tem? **RONR 554**
54-4	A.	The second item of business at a meeting to organize a permanent organization.
	Q.	What is elect a secretary pro tem? **RONR 554**
54-5	A.	Business which usually follows the election of the secretary.
	Q.	What is providing background information? **RONR 554**
54-6	A.	The type of the usual first resolution at a meeting to organize a permanent organization.
	Q.	What is resolution of intention to form a society? **RONR 554-55**
54-7	A.	It gets the process started, but it does not bring the organization into being.
	Q.	What is resolution of intention to form a society? **RONR 555**
54-8	A.	Two actions required to bring an organization into being.
	Q.	What is adoption of bylaws and signing of membership roll? **RONR 555**
54-9	A.	Adoption of a motion that a committee be appointed to draft bylaws.
	Q.	What is the first step following a motion of intention? **RONR 555**
54-10	A.	Adoption of a motion setting the time and place for the next meeting of the group looking to form this new organization.
	Q.	What is the second step following a motion of intention? **RONR 555**
54-11	A.	The third step usually taken at the first organizational meeting after adoption of the resolution of intent.
	Q.	What are introduction of motions to authorize reproduction of draft bylaws? **RONR 555-56**

54-12	A.	Other business which may have taken place at the first organizational meeting.
	Q.	What is informal discussion of aims and structure of the proposed society? **RONR 556**
54-13	A.	It is often helpful to the bylaws committee of a new organization to procure and study these.
	Q.	What are bylaws of similar organizations? **RONR 556**
54-14	A.	It is advisable that the bylaws committee of a new organization consult one of these.
	Q.	What is a professional parliamentarian? **RONR 556**
54-15	A.	The need to do this should be considered by the bylaws committee for a new organization, particularly if it intends to own real estate, become a beneficiary to a will, engage employees, and the like.
	Q.	What is incorporate the organization? **RONR 556**
54-16	A.	If the new organization needs to incorporate, the person the bylaws committee is advised to consult.
	Q.	What is an attorney? **RONR 557**
54-17	A.	The officers who start off the second organizational meeting.
	Q.	What is the president pro tem and secretary pro tem elected at the first meeting? **RONR 557**
54-18	A.	The first item of business at the second organizational meeting.
	Q.	What is reading and adoption of minutes of the first meeting? **RONR 557**
54-19	A.	The usual second item of business at the second organizational meeting.
	Q.	What is consideration and adoption of bylaws? **RONR 557**
54-20	A.	A document considered before the bylaws are considered.
	Q.	What is the corporate charter? RONR 557
54-21	A.	The method for consideration of proposed bylaws for a new organization.
	Q.	What is by article or paragraph? **RONR 558**
54-22	A.	If the need for important additions or amendments becomes desirable but additional time or investigation is required for their preparation.
	Q.	What is a motion to recommit the proposed bylaws with instructions that the committee report at another meeting for which the time can be fixed? **RONR 559**

54-23	A.	The vote required to adopt bylaws that bring an organization into being.	
	Q.	What is only a majority?	**RONR 559**
54-24	A.	The time the adopted bylaws for a new organization take effect.	
	Q.	What is immediately?	**RONR 559**
54-25	A.	After adoption of bylaws for a new organization, only these are entitled to vote.	
	Q.	What are those who join the society?	**RONR 559**
54-26	A.	Status of meeting as initial members enroll.	
	Q.	What is recess?	**RONR 559**
54-27	A.	Used to identify initial members of a new society.	
	Q.	What is a signed permanent record sheet?	**RONR 559-60**
54-28	A.	A commitment to prompt payment of the initiation fee (if there is one) and dues for the first year.	
	Q.	What is signing permanent record sheet?	**RONR 560**
54-29	A.	Person collecting fees and dues during the signing of the permanent record sheet.	
	Q.	What is the secretary pro tem?	**RONR 560**
54-30	A.	Action which occurs following enrollment of "charter" members and reading of that roll.	
	Q.	What is election of permanent officers?	**RONR 560**
54-31	A.	The time when permanent officers replace officers pro tem.	
	Q.	What is immediately following declaration of election?	**RONR 560**
54-32	A.	Often required to allow the president to name committees and committee chairmen.	
	Q.	What is an adjourned meeting?	**RONR 560-61**
54-33	A.	Sometimes essential to be done at end of the second (or third) organizational meeting.	
	Q.	What is to name the chairmen of certain committees?	**RONR 561**

Section 55 - Merger, Consolidation, and Dissolution of Societies

Robert's Rules of Order Newly Revised, 11th Edition - Pages 561-64

55-1	A.	The two terms that apply to combining of societies.	
	Q.	What are merger and consolidation?	**RONR 561**
55-2	A.	The term for when one of the two combining organizations continues and the other loses its independent identity.	
	Q.	What is a merger?	**RONR 561**
55-3	A.	The term for when a new organization is formed by the combining of two organizations.	
	Q.	What is a consolidation?	**RONR 561**
55-4	A.	Something the resulting organization of a merger or a consolidation may acquire.	
	Q.	What is a new name?	**RONR 562**
55-5	A.	A person who should be consulted when either of the combining organizations is incorporated.	
	Q.	What is an attorney?	**RONR 562**
55-6	A.	The two actions required of the organization losing its separate identity in a merger.	
	Q.	What is adopts a resolution to merge and adopt a resolution(s) transferring assets and liabilities to other organization?	**RONR 562**
55-7	A.	The notice and vote required for the resolution to merge.	
	Q.	What is same as required to amend the organization's bylaws?	**RONR 562**
55-8	A.	In a merger, the surviving organization takes this action.	
	Q.	What is adopts resolution accepting the other organization?	**RONR 562**
55-9	A.	Notice and vote required for accepting the other organization in a merger.	
	Q.	What is same as to amend surviving organization's bylaws?	**RONR 562**
55-10	A.	In a consolidation, each organization takes this action.	
	Q.	What is adopts a resolution of consolidation?	**RONR 563**
55-11	A.	The required action on bylaws when a merger of two organizations occurs.	
	Q.	What is none?	**RONR 563**

55-12	A.	The required action on bylaws when a consolidation of two organizations occurs.	
	Q.	What is new bylaws much be adopted?	**RONR 563**
55-13	A.	Action to be taken when an organization is no longer needed.	
	Q.	What is disband or dissolve?	**RONR 563**
55-14	A.	The person who should be consulted in the dissolution of an incorporated society.	
	Q.	What is an attorney?	**RONR 563-64**
55-15	A.	The action to dissolve an unincorporated society.	
	Q.	What is adopt a resolution to dissolve?	**RONR 564**
55-16	A.	The notice and vote required for a resolution to dissolve.	
	Q.	What is same as to amend organization's bylaws?	**RONR 564**
55-17	A.	The effect of the adoption of a resolution to dissolve.	
	Q.	What is to rescind the bylaws?	**RONR 564**

CHAPTER XVIII: BYLAWS

Section 56 - Basic Classification; Order of Precedence of Motions
Robert's Rules of Order Newly Revised, 11th Edition - Pages 565-91

56-1	A. Q.	The document which contains basic rules that relate to itself as an organization. What is the bylaws (and/or constitution)? ***RONR 565***
56-2	A. Q.	The content of this document has important bearing on the rights and duties of members within an organization. What is the bylaws? ***RONR 566***
56-3	A. Q.	The body that has the full and sole power to act for the entire organization and does so by majority vote except as the rules of the organization provide otherwise. What is definition of an assembly? ***RONR 566***
56-4	A. Q.	The ways that limitations or standing delegation of assembly's power is made. What is by provision in the bylaws? ***RONR 566***
56-5	A. Q.	Appointed at first organizational meeting or when a society wishes to undertake a general revision of its bylaws. What is a bylaws committee? ***RONR 566***
56-6	A. Q. Q. Q. Q. Q.	Suggested composition for a committee to draw up bylaws. What is large? What is consists of most judicious persons available? What is those who have a special interest in the rules? What is includes those who would consume much time in discussion when presented to assembly? What is persons having writing ability of the kind required? ***RONR 566***
56-7	A. Q.	A person who can be of assistance in drafting a set of bylaws. What is a professional parliamentarian? ***RONR 566***
56-8	A. Q.	The document an attorney should be consulted to draft if the society is to be incorporated. What is a corporate charter (articles of incorporation)? ***RONR 567***
56-9	A. Q.	The document the bylaws committee should review when preparing a revision. What are the current bylaws? ***RONR 567***

56-10	A.	Documents of similar organizations or other subordinate units.
	Q.	What is should be reviewed? **RONR 567**
56-11	A.	Documents the bylaws committee should review when the organization is a subordinate unit of a larger organization.
	Q.	What are the parent organization's (superior body's) bylaws? **RONR 567**
56-12	A.	Provisions in the bylaws of the superior body without local application.
	Q.	What is should not be included in the subordinate unit's bylaws? **RONR 567-68**
56-13	A.	Often used by the bylaw committee when bylaws are expected to be long and complex.
	Q.	What is subcommittees? **RONR 568**
56-14	A.	Used to eliminate inconsistencies, make the style uniform, and make sure everything relating to a single subject is placed in the same or adjacent articles.
	Q.	What is a final review subcommittee? **RONR 568**
56-15	A.	Indisputability of meaning and application is more important than this.
	Q.	What is readability? **RONR 568**
56-16	A.	In bylaws, the manner in which each sentence should be written.
	Q.	What is impossible to quote out of context? **RONR 568-69**
56-17	A.	In bylaws, the place where exceptions or qualifications should be included.
	Q.	What is within the sentence to which they apply? **RONR 569**
56-18	A.	Should be included if the exceptions cannot be included within a sentence.
	Q.	What is an allusion or reference to any exception? **RONR 569**
56-19	A.	The method that an assembly usually uses to consider new bylaws and revisions of existing bylaws.
	Q.	What is to consider seriatim (article by article, and section by section)? **RONR 569**
56-20	A.	A provision that may be included in a motion to adopt revised bylaws.
	Q.	What are provisos? **RONR 569-70**
56-21	A.	The vote required to adopt a revision to the present bylaws.
	Q.	What is vote required to amend the existing bylaws? **RONR 570**

56-22 A.	The vote required to adopt new bylaws to establish an organization.	
Q.	What is a majority vote?	*RONR 570*
56-23 A.	The usual way that articles in the bylaws are designated.	
Q.	What is by Roman numerals.	*RONR 570*
56-24 A.	The usual way that sections within an article in the bylaws are designated.	
Q.	What is by Arabic numerals?	*RONR 570*
56-25 A.	The usual title for the first article in the bylaws.	
Q.	What is Name?	*RONR 570*
56-26 A.	Suggested content of the first article in the bylaws of an unincorporated society.	
Q.	What is full, exact, and properly punctuated name of the society?	*RONR 570*
56-27 A.	Place where the official name appears in incorporated organizations,	
Q.	What is corporate charter?	*RONR 570*
56-28 A.	The official name of an organization when there is a conflict between the name that appears in the corporate charter and the one in the bylaws.	
Q.	What is name as listed in the corporate charter [superior document]?	*RONR 570*
56-29 A.	In unincorporated societies, this is usually the second article in the bylaws.	
Q.	What is the object of the society?	*RONR 571*
56-30 A.	The manner in which the society's object should be presented in the bylaws article.	
Q.	What is concisely expressed in a single sentence?	*RONR 571*
56-31 A.	When the society has several objectives, the form in which they should be presented in the bylaws article.	
Q.	What is as phrases separated by semicolons?	*RONR 571*
56-32 A.	The reason for the object statement in the bylaws being general in nature.	
Q.	What is it sets boundaries within which business can be introduced at meetings.	*RONR 571*
56-33 A.	Circumstance where the object article can be omitted from the bylaws.	
Q.	What is when it appears in the article of incorporation?	*RONR 571*

56-34	A.	Device sometime used when the object stated in the articles of incorporation no longer states its object in modern terms or with the specificity now desired.
	Q.	What is including the object as a preamble to the bylaws? **RONR 571**

56-35	A.	Typically the third article of the bylaws deals with this aspect of the society.
	Q.	What is members? **RONR 571**

56-36	A.	Classes, such as "active," "associate," and the like, appear in this place in the bylaws.
	Q.	What is article on members? **RONR 571**

56-37	A.	Place in bylaws to find membership qualification or eligibility.
	Q.	What is article on members? **RONR 571**

56-38	A.	Where to find: required fees and dues, the date(s) when payable, the time and prescribed procedure for notifying members if they become delinquent in payment, and the date on which a member will be dropped for nonpayment
	Q.	What is article on members in bylaws? **RONR 571**

56-39	A.	Must be included in the bylaws before a member's voting rights can be suspended for being in the arrears on his dues.
	Q.	What is a provision to permit this? **RONR 571-72**

56-40	A.	Must be included in the bylaws before a member can be assessed any additional payments aside from their dues.
	Q.	What is a provision to permit this? **RONR 572**

56-41	A.	Suggested when the financial obligations are very complicated.
	Q.	What is including them in a separate article? **RONR 572**

56-42	A.	Must be included in the bylaws to make attendance at a certain proportion of the meetings a requirement for continued membership.
	Q.	What is a provision to require this? **RONR 572**

56-43	A.	The word "members" sometimes refers to these rather than to persons.
	Q.	What are local units, or constituent clubs? **RONR 572**

56-44	A.	The usual bylaw article which follows the article on members.
	Q.	What is officers? **RONR 572**

56-45	A.	The order in which the officers should be listed in the bylaws article on officers.
	Q.	What is by rank, the president should be listed first? **RONR 572**

56-46	A.	The usual bylaw classification for directors.
	Q.	What is as officers? **RONR 572**
56-47	A.	The phrase suggested to be included to ensure all normal duties are covered in bylaws article on officers' duties.
	Q.	What is "... and such other duties applicable to the office as prescribed by the parliamentary authority adopted by the Society?" **RONR 572**
56-48	A.	Suggested method for dealing with the situation where the extraordinarily duties of the officers are numerous.
	Q.	What is collecting all of them in a separate article? **RONR 572**
56-49	A.	Causes repetition of duties and may occasionally result in problems of interpretation.
	Q.	What is collecting all of them in a separate article? **RONR 572-73**
56-50	A.	The usual place in the bylaws for specifying a nominating committee and its operation.
	Q.	What is article on officers? **RONR 573**
56-51	A.	Wording which allows the nominating committee to nominate more than one candidate for an office.
	Q.	What is "the committee shall nominate candidates for each office"? **RONR 573**
56-52	A.	Bylaws wording that imposes a limit on the nominating committee to nominate a single candidate for each office.
	Q.	What is "the committee shall nominate a candidate for each office"? **RONR 573**
56-53	A.	The location where the process for election of officers and the term of office are usually found in the bylaws.
	Q.	What is article on officers? **RONR 573**
56-54	A.	When there is only one candidate for an office, a provision sometimes found in the bylaws.
	Q.	What is to dispense with the ballot vote? **RONR 573**
56-55	A.	The privilege that members are deprived of when the bylaws provide for dispensing with the ballot when there is only a single candidate for an office.
	Q.	What is voting for "write-in" candidates? **RONR 573**
56-56	A.	Must be included in the bylaws for an election to be conducted by mail, by plurality vote, by preferential voting, or by cumulative voting.
	Q.	What is a provision to permit this? **RONR 573**

Here is the Answer! What is the Question? Book 5

163

56-57 A.	Happens unless the bylaws specify when their term begins.	
Q.	What is assume office at the instant the chair declares each officer elected?	**RONR 573**
56-58 A.	Possible problem for the society if bylaws specifies a fixed length for the term.	
Q.	What is could find itself without any officers?	**RONR 573-74**
56-59 A.	To be able to remove an officer only for cause or at the pleasure of the membership.	
Q.	What is consideration when establishing term length?	**RONR 574**
56-60 A.	The phrase to use for the case where removal is only for cause.	
Q.	What is "... term of X years and until their successors are elected"?	**RONR 574**
56-61 A.	The phrase to use for the case where removal is at the pleasure of the membership.	
Q.	What is "... term of X years or until their successors are elected"?	**RONR 574**
56-62 A.	"Officers may be removed from office for cause by disciplinary proceedings as provided in the parliamentary authority."	
Q.	What is explanatory sentence which can be used to help members understand the use of "and" in the term length?	**RONR 574**
56-63 A.	"Officers may be removed from office at the pleasure of the membership as provided in the parliamentary authority."	
Q.	What is explanatory sentence which can be used to help members understand the use of "or" in the term length?	**RONR 574**
56-64 A.	The usual place to find the requirement for limiting the number of terms an officer can serve.	
Q.	What is bylaws article on officers?	**RONR 574-75**
56-65 A.	The condition under which a person is considered to have served a term in office.	
Q.	What is served more than half a term?	**RONR 575**
56-66 A.	The place to find the requirements for filling a vacancy in any office.	
Q.	What is in the bylaws article on officers?	**RONR 575**
56-67 A.	The person who fills a vacancy in the office of president when there is no bylaws provision.	
Q.	What is the vice-president (or first vice-president)?	**RONR 575**
56-68 A.	The usual bylaws article following the one on officers.	
Q.	What is meetings?	**RONR 575**

56-69	A.	Information the bylaws article on meetings should provide for the regular meetings.
	Q.	What is fix the day on which regular meetings are to be held? **RONR 575**

56-70	A.	When the bylaws include in the article on meetings "unless otherwise ordered by the Society."
	Q.	What is how the bylaws allow for the change of the date for a single meeting? **RONR 575**

56-71	A.	Concerning regular meetings, the hour and place at which meetings are to be held.
	Q.	What is should not be included in the bylaws but rather in a standing rule? **RONR 575**

56-72	A.	In the article on meetings, the purpose for which one of the regular meetings should be designated.
	Q.	What is specify it as the annual meeting? **RONR 576**

56-73	A.	Business usually conducted at an annual meeting which differs from the business at the regular meeting.
	Q.	What are officers are elected and annual reports are received? **RONR 576**

56-74	A.	Required to be included in the bylaws before a special meeting can be called.
	Q.	What is a provision to permit this? **RONR 576**

56-75	A.	Should be included in the bylaw provision on special meetings.
	Q.	What are who can call the meeting and the number of days' notice required? **RONR 576**

56-76	A.	A provision often include in bylaws for special meetings (although not needed).
	Q.	What is no business shall be transacted except that mentioned in the call? **RONR 576**

56-77	A.	The section in the bylaws were the quorum requirement should be established.
	Q.	What is the article on meetings? **RONR 576**

56-78	A.	An article required in bylaws to establish a smaller group to administer the society's business between regular meetings.
	Q.	What is article on the executive board (or board of directors)? **RONR 576**

56-79	A.	Information the bylaws article should specify concerning the executive board.
	Q.	What are composition, powers, and special rules? **RONR 576-77**
56-80	A.	The usual name for the small assembly designated to act for the organization between meetings.
	Q.	What is executive board? **RONR 577**
56-81	A.	The usual name used instead of "executive board" when there is to be a smaller body of the board.
	Q.	What is the board of directors? **RONR 577**
56-82	A.	The usual name of the smaller body within the Board of Directors when there is one.
	Q.	What is executive committee? **RONR 577**
56-83	A.	Place where the executive committee is established and authority identified.
	Q.	What is in an article following the article on the board of directors? **RONR 577**
56-84	A.	"Board of Managers," "Board of Trustees," "Board of Governors," and "Administrative Council."
	Q.	What are other names for the "Executive Board" or "Board of Directors"? **RONR 577**
56-85	A.	Board's power to alter a decision of the society's assembly.
	Q.	What is none unless specifically authorized in bylaws? **RONR 577**
56-86	A.	Power limited to supervise and implementation of the decisions of the society's assembly, and to attend to any business that cannot wait until the next meeting.
	Q.	What is frequently provided in bylaws? **RONR 577-78**
56-87	A.	Can be provided to leave the entire administrative authority of the society to the board between the society's meetings.
	Q.	What is full power? **RONR 578**
56-88	A.	The article which usually follows the article on executive board in bylaws.
	Q.	What is committees? **RONR 578**
56-89	A.	Term for the permanent committees which should be identified in the bylaws in the article on committees.
	Q.	What is standing committees? **RONR 578**

56-90	A.	Information which should be included in the bylaws in a separate section for each standing committee.
	Q.	What is name, composition, manner of selection, and duties? **RONR 578**

56-91	A.	A requirement that must be included for there to be standing committees other than those specifically named in the bylaws.
	Q.	What is a bylaw provision permitting the establishment of such other standing committees as are deemed necessary? **RONR 578**

56-92	A.	Required when all business of a certain class is to be automatically referred to a standing committee.
	Q.	What is a bylaw provision or special rule of order? **RONR 578**

56-93	A.	The number of standing committees that a local unit should have.
	Q.	What is as few as needed? **RONR 579**

56-94	A.	When the nominating committee is a standing committee, it is usually listed in this location on the bylaws.
	Q.	What is in the article on officers? **RONR 579**

56-95	A.	Required for the president to appoint all special committees.
	Q.	What is a bylaw provision authorizing this? **RONR 579**

56-96	A.	The bylaw provision which empowers the president to appoint such special committees as the society directs does NOT include this power.
	Q.	What is the power to appoint committees on his own initiative? **RONR 579**

56-97	A.	Required if the president is to be authorized to appoint non-assembly members to committees without assembly approval.
	Q.	What is a bylaw provision authorizing? **RONR 579**

56-98	A.	Required for the president to participate in the committees of the organization.
	Q.	What is a bylaw provision making him an ex officio member of the committees? **RONR 579**

56-99	A.	Rights and duties which comes with the president's being an ex officio member of a committee.
	Q.	What is right to participate and vote, but no duty to attend meetings? **RONR 579**

56-100	A.	Standing committee for which the president should not be an ex officio member.
	Q.	What is the nominating committee? **RONR 579**

56-101A.	Committees which is a good idea to exclude from the president being an ex officio member.
Q.	What are committees dealing with discipline and the nominating committee? *RONR 579-80*

56-102A.	The usual method to provide the society with a set of standard rules of order.
Q.	What is an article in bylaws prescribing the parliamentary authority? *RONR 580*

56-103A.	Can be adopted to supplement the parliamentary authority.
Q.	What are special rules of order? *RONR 580*

56-104A.	Condition when the parliamentary authority requires any alteration to a rule to be placed in the bylaws.
Q.	What is cannot be placed in the special rules of order? *RONR 580*

56-105A.	The position of what another parliamentary authority says on a point which is covered by the parliamentary authority designated in the bylaws.
Q.	What is is of no authority? *RONR 580*

56-106A.	The position of other parliamentary authorities when the parliamentary authority designated in the bylaws does not cover the point.
Q.	What is may be persuasive but is not binding upon the society? *RONR 580*

56-107A.	Bylaws should always have this article allowing for changes.
Q.	What is article on amendment of bylaws? *RONR 580-81*

56-108A.	The minimum requirements suggested for amendment of bylaws.
Q.	What is advance notice and approval by two-thirds vote? *RONR 581*

56-109A.	The requirements to amend bylaws which do not contain provisions for their amendment.
Q.	What is previous notice and a two-thirds vote, or, without notice, a vote of the majority of the entire membership? *RONR 581*

56-110A.	The reason for suggesting the use of "the previous meeting" instead of "a previous meeting."
Q.	What is "a" would permit indefinite delay and would defeat the purpose of giving notice? *RONR 581*

56-111A.	In addition to alerting the members to the change, amendments to the proposed bylaw amendment is restricted to changes within the scope of the notice.
Q.	What is done by advance notice? *RONR 581 (also see 594-96)*

56-112A.	Manner prescribed for giving notice.
Q.	What is as specified in bylaws, suitable to the needs of the particular assembly? **RONR 581**
56-113A.	When there is no specified time for the advance notice in the bylaws and a committee is appointed to revise the bylaws, the bylaw revision can be acted upon at this time.
Q.	What is when the committee reports since the action of appointing the committee is considered the notice? **RONR 581**
56-114A.	When there is a requirement for advance notice at the previous meeting and a committee is appointed to revise the bylaws, the bylaw revision can be acted upon at this time.
Q.	What is at the meeting after the meeting when the committee reports? **RONR 581**
56-115A.	When a society has frequent meetings, the manner in which it is often advisable to restrict consideration of bylaw amendments.
Q.	What is only at a quarterly business meeting or an annual meeting? **RONR 581-82**
56-116A.	The advance notice requirement for societies holding only one meeting a year or less often.
Q.	What is sent by mail to member delegates or constituent societies? **RONR 582**
56-117A.	The requirements to amend a constitution, when a society has a constitution separate from the bylaws.
Q.	What is should be more difficult to amend than the bylaws? **RONR 582**
56-118A.	The problem with using the phrase "a vote of two-thirds of the members" in connection with amending the bylaws.
Q.	What is two-thirds of all the membership would rarely be present at a meeting? **RONR 582**
56-119A.	"Amend, alter, add to, or repeal," or "alter or amend," or "amend or in any way change."
Q.	What are phrases which are redundant and should be avoided? **RONR 582**
56-120A.	The suggestion concerning defining the term "two-third vote" in the bylaws.
Q.	What is should be avoided since these definitions are found in the parliamentary authority? **RONR 582**
56-121A.	Additional articles in a society's bylaws.
Q.	What is include as needed? **RONR 582**

56-122A.	The statement: "Each society decided for itself the meaning of its by-laws."
Q.	What is one of the principles of interpretation of bylaws? ***RONR 588***

56-123A.	When the meaning of a bylaw provision is clear, the way the society can change that meaning.
Q.	What is only by amending its bylaws? ***RONR 588***

56-124A.	The problem that must exist in order for a society to have occasion to interpret its bylaws.
Q.	What is an ambiguity? ***RONR 588***

56-125A.	The manner in which any ambiguity in the bylaws must be interpreted.
Q.	What is in harmony with the other bylaws? ***RONR 588***

56-126A.	As far as it can be determined, information that should be used to help interpret an ambiguous bylaw provision.
Q.	What is intention of society at the time the bylaw was adopted? ***RONR 588***

56-127A.	Vote required to adopt an interpretation of an ambiguous bylaw provision.
Q.	What is a majority vote? ***RONR 588-89***

56-128A.	Action that should be taken on any ambiguous bylaw provision.
Q.	What is amended as soon as practicable? ***RONR 589***

56-129A.	The statement: "When a provision of the bylaws is susceptible to two meanings, one of which conflicts with or renders absurd another by-law provision, and the other meaning does not, the latter must be taken as the true meaning."
Q.	What is a principle for interpretation of bylaws? ***RONR 589***

56-130A.	The statement: "A general statement or rule is always of less authority than a specific statement or rule and yields to it."
Q.	What is a principle for interpretation of bylaws? ***RONR 589***

56-131A.	The person that has the right to quote a general statement as of authority against a specific statement in the bylaws.
Q.	What is no one? ***RONR 589***

56-132A.	The statement: "If the bylaws authorize certain things specifically, other things of the same class are thereby prohibited."
Q.	What is a principle for interpretation of bylaws? ***RONR 589***

56-133A.	The presumption concerning things placed into the bylaws.
Q.	What is they are not included without some reason? ***RONR 589-90***

56-134 A.	The presumption that when the bylaws authorize certain action to be done that can clearly be done without the authorization of the by-laws.
Q.	What is that all others of the same class are prohibited? **RONR 590**
56-135 A.	The statement: "A provision granting certain privileges carries with it a right to a part of the privileges, but prohibits a greater privilege."
Q.	What is a principle for interpretation of bylaws? **RONR 590**
56-136 A.	The statement: "A prohibition or limitation prohibits everything greater than what is prohibited, or that goes beyond the limitation; but it permits what is less than the limitation; and also permits things of the same class that are not mentioned in the prohibition or limitation and that are evidently not improper."
Q.	What is a principle for interpretation of bylaws? **RONR 590**
56-137 A.	The statement: "The imposition of a definite penalty for a particular action prohibits the increase or diminution of the penalty."
Q.	What is a principle for interpretation of bylaws? **RONR 591**
56-138 A.	The statement: "In cases where the bylaws use a general term and also two or more specific terms that are wholly included under the general one, a rule in which only the general term is used applies to all the specific terms."
Q.	What is a principle for interpretation of bylaws? **RONR 591**

Section 57 – Amendment of Bylaws

Robert's Rules of Order Newly Revised, 11th Edition - Pages 592-99

57-1	A.	The motion to amend the bylaws is a particular case of this motion.
	Q.	What is Amend Something Previously Adopted? **_RONR 592_**
57-2	A.	A motion to amend the bylaws comes under the same rules as this class of motion with a few exceptions.
	Q.	What is a main motion? **_RONR 592_**
57-3	A.	The bylaws usually provide for these special requirements for a motion to amend the bylaws.
	Q.	What is notice and a two-thirds vote? **_RONR 592_**
57-4	A.	The restriction on primary and secondary amendments to a motion to amend the bylaws.
	Q.	What is limited by the extent of change for which notice was given? **_RONR 592_**
57-5	A.	As opposed to a main motion, the way the reconsideration of a motion to amend the bylaws is limited.
	Q.	What is an affirmative vote cannot be reconsidered? **_RONR 592_**
57-6	A.	The rule that no other conflicting main motion is in order thereafter in the same meeting.
	Q.	What is not applicable to amendments to bylaws? **_RONR 592_**
57-7	A.	An isolated change is to be made in the bylaws.
	Q.	What is can be treated as any motion to Amend Something Previously Adopted? **_RONR 592-93_**
57-8	A.	The rule of scope of notice when a section contains several isolated changes but is presented as a substitute amendment.
	Q.	What is restricted to only those areas specifically changed? **_RONR 593_**
57-9	A.	Status of words not changed when a section is presented as the amendment to the bylaws.
	Q.	What is not subject to amendment? **_RONR 593_**
57-10	A.	The term applied to a proposed substitution of the bylaws with an entirely new set of bylaws.
	Q.	What is a revision? **_RONR 593_**
57-11	A.	Can be perfected by first-degree and second-degree amendments when a revision to the bylaws is proposed.
	Q.	What is the entire document? **_RONR 593_**

57-12 A.	Happens if the proposed revision to the bylaws is rejected.	
Q.	What is current bylaws continue in effect?	**RONR 593**
57-13 A.	Method of dealing with a revision or lengthy amendment involving more than one section.	
Q.	What is seriatim?	**RONR 593**
57-14 A.	When there are several proposed amendments to the bylaws which are in conflict with each other, the chair should do this.	
Q.	What is arrange them in logical order, like filling the blank?	**RONR 594**
57-15 A.	When considering conflicting bylaw amendments, the logical order for consideration.	
Q.	What is taking the least inclusive amendment first?	**RONR 594**
57-16 A.	When a series of conflicting bylaw amendments are considered, the one which takes effect.	
Q.	What is the last (most inclusive) one adopted?	**RONR 594**
57-17 A.	The right of the proposer of a bylaw amendment not yet considered which is in conflict with an amendment just adopted.	
Q.	What is to have his proposal considered?	**RONR 594**
57-18A.	When a proposed bylaw amendment (in a series of conflicting amendments) which modifies words which have been removed by a previously adopted amendment.	
Q.	What is the proposed amendment is dropped?	**RONR 594**
57-19 A.	Type of vote taken as the final vote on any bylaw amendment unless it is nearly unanimous.	
Q.	What is a counted vote (recorded in the minutes)?	**RONR 594**
57-20 A.	A proposed bylaw amendment can have these types of amendments applied to it.	
Q.	What is both first degree and second degree?	**RONR 594**
57-21 A.	Amendments to a proposed bylaw amendment that are out of order.	
Q.	What is one which increases the modification of the article or rule to be amended?	**RONR 595**
57-22 A.	Amendments to a proposed bylaw amendment presented as a modified section which are out of order.	
Q.	What is one which affects parts of the section not proposed to be amended?	**RONR 595**

57-23	A.	If the proposed bylaw amendment is to strike out a section, the status of a proposed amendment to that amendment to change the words in the existing bylaws.
	Q.	What is out of order? ***RONR 595-96***
57-24	A.	Action of members who want to retain an existing part in the bylaws but with some changes when an amendment is proposed to strike out the part.
	Q.	What is immediately give notice of their amendments to the existing part? ***RONR 595-96***
57-25	A.	Unless restricted by the bylaws, this person can propose an amendment to the bylaws.
	Q.	What is any member? ***RONR 596***
57-26	A.	Place in the order of business when an oral notice of a bylaw amendment is made.
	Q.	What is during new business? ***RONR 596***
57-27	A.	When notice of a bylaw amendment is required to be by mail, the group that is responsible for paying the cost of sending such notice.
	Q.	What is the society (not the member or committee proposing the amendment)? ***RONR 596***
57-28	A.	Order of business heading under which a bylaw amendment, on which notice has been given, is considered.
	Q.	What is Unfinished Business and General Orders? ***RONR 596***
57-29	A.	A good device of presentation of bylaw amendments which ensures members understand the extent of the change.
	Q.	What is existing bylaw and the bylaw with the proposed changes in parallel columns with the formal motion over the top of the two columns? ***RONR 596***
57-30	A.	Time that an adopted bylaw amendment goes into effect.
	Q.	What is immediately? ***RONR 597***
57-31	A.	The term used for a provision changing the time when a bylaw amendment takes effect.
	Q.	What is a proviso? ***RONR 597***
57-32	A.	The two methods by which a proviso can be attached to a bylaw amendment.
	Q.	What is by an amendment to the enacting words of the motion to amend or while the amendment is pending, by the adoption of an incidental motion? ***RONR 597***

57-33	A.	The vote required to attach a proviso to a bylaw amendment.
	Q.	What is a majority vote? **RONR 597**
57-34	A.	The preferred method to handle temporary changes or the mechanics of a transition.
	Q.	What is a proviso? **RONR 597**
57-35	A.	A problem concerning changes to the bylaws article on officers.
	Q.	What is the current officer holder may be affected unless the amendment includes a proviso stating otherwise? **RONR 597**
57-36	A.	Consideration to be taken when making changes to the article on officers in the bylaws.
	Q.	What is that a virtual contract exists between the society and it officers which should be taken into account? **RONR 597-98**
57-37	A.	The time when a bylaw amendment becomes part of the bylaws, even if it doesn't take effect until later.
	Q.	What is immediately? **RONR 598**
57-38	A.	Indication in bylaws when a change does not take effect until a later time.
	Q.	What is a footnote indication when it takes effect? **RONR 598**
57-39	A.	The group who can change caption and headings, which could have any effect on meaning.
	Q.	What is only the assembly? **RONR 598**
57-40	A.	Changes and corrections concerning article and section numbers or cross- references which cannot result in a change of meaning.
	Q.	What is can be delegated to the secretary or a committee? **RONR 598-99**
57-41	A.	The method of delegating the making of editorial changes to the by-laws.
	Q.	What is adoption of a main motion (resolution)? **RONR 599**

CHAPTER XIX: CONVENTIONS

Section 58 – Conventions of Delegates

Robert's Rules of Order Newly Revised, 11th Edition - Pages 600-07

58-1	A.	Name for an assembly of delegates.	
	Q.	What is a convention?	**RONR 600**
58-2	A.	Chosen as the representatives of the constituent units or subdivisions within a larger group of people.	
	Q.	What are delegates?	**RONR 600**
58-3	A.	Sometimes known as congress, conference, convocation, general assembly, house of delegates, or house of representatives.	
	Q.	What is a convention?	**RONR 600**
58-4	A.	The term often applied to the body of delegates of learned or professional associations.	
	Q.	What is house of delegates or house of representatives?	**RONR 600**
58-5	A.	Other activities sometimes held at a convention.	
	Q.	What is seminars, workshops, educational and social activities?	**RONR 600**
58-6	A.	A body of delegates who are elected for a fixed term during which they hold sessions from time to time as prescribed in the bylaws.	
	Q.	What is House of Delegates or House of Representatives?	**RONR 600-01**
58-7	A.	Sometimes called for the purpose of forming an association or federation.	
	Q.	What is a convention?	**RONR 601**
58-8	A.	Document which authorizes a periodic convention.	
	Q.	What is the bylaws or other governing documents?	**RONR 601**
58-9	A.	Bylaw provisions which should be made concerning delegates.	
	Q.	What is qualifications, basis for determining number, and method for electing?	**RONR 602**
58-10	A.	Condition for a constituent unit to be in good standing.	
	Q.	What is should be specified in bylaws?	**RONR 602**
58-11	A.	The number of delegates to which a unit shall be entitled.	
	Q.	What is should be specified in bylaws?	**RONR 602**

58-12	A.	To avoid a change of officers during the convention, bylaws should specify when newly elected officers take up their duties.
	Q.	What is at the close of the convention? **RONR 602**

58-13	A.	Ways voting membership of a convention is established.
	Q.	What is accredited delegates elected by a constituent body?
	Q.	What is through provisions in bylaws?
	Q.	What is being an incumbent elective officer?
	Q.	What is elected alternate replacing a delegate? **RONR 602-03**

58-14	A.	Generally replaces a constituent unit's president if unable to attend convention.
	Q.	What is vice-president (or first vice-president)? **RONR 603**

58-15	A.	A replacement for a delegate when the delegate is unable to attend or must leave early from a convention.
	Q.	What is an alternate? **RONR 603**

58-16	A.	Serves as delegate if president unable to attend.
	Q.	What is vice-president (or ranking officer)? **RONR 603**

58-17	A.	Qualifications for an alternate.
	Q.	What is same as for a delegate? **RONR 604**

58-18	A.	The way the proper alternate delegate is determined.
	Q.	What is the order in which elected? **RONR 604**

58-19	A.	A way used to match delegates and alternates.
	Q.	What is pairing? **RONR 604**

58-20	A.	The process for an alternate to replace a delegate.
	Q.	What is credentials committee is presented with evidence of a delegate's withdrawal and the alternate is re-registered as the new delegate? **RONR 605**

58-21	A.	The requirement of a delegate who is leaving a convention.
	Q.	What is to notify the credentials committee so the alternate can be properly accredited? **RONR 605**

58-22	A.	The requirement for an alternate to temporarily substitute for a delegate.
	Q.	What is must be specified in the bylaws? **RONR 605**

58-23	A.	The duties of a delegate.
	Q.	What is attend the convention, be present at business meetings, and to report to his unit what transpired? **RONR 605**

58-24	A.	A delegate's voting status, unless instructed.
	Q.	What is free to vote as he sees fit? **RONR 605**
58-25	A.	The name for group of delegates meeting outside of the convention.
	Q.	What is a caucus? **RONR 605**
58-26	A.	The rules usually used in a caucus.
	Q.	What are committee rules? **RONR 606**
58-27	A.	Usually serves as chairman of a delegation from one unit.
	Q.	What is the unit's president? **RONR 606**
58-28	A.	Serves as chairman of a delegation in the absence of the president or vice-president.
	Q.	What is a chairman selected as outlined for the case of any committee? **RONR 606**
58-29	A.	The requirement concerning instructed delegates when this instruction is known to the convention's chairman.
	Q.	What is must be enforced on the delegate? **RONR 606**

59-1	A.	The three committees which do the principle parliamentary functions for a convention.
	Q.	What are credentials committee, committee on standing rules, and program committee? **RONR 607**
59-2	A.	Prepare and certifies to the convention the list of officers, delegates, and alternates that it has registered.
	Q.	What is the credentials committee? **RONR 607**
59-3	A.	Drafts rules of operating procedure specially required for the particular convention.
	Q.	What is the committee on standing rules? **RONR 607**
59-4	A.	Plans a convention program combining a suitable order of business with special features.
	Q.	What is the program committee? **RONR 607**
59-5	A.	The committee who secures the hall, hotel accommodations, and related services.
	Q.	What is convention arrangements committee? **RONR 608**
59-6	A.	The committee responsible for the review of resolutions and original main motions.
	Q.	What is the resolutions committee? **RONR 608**
59-7	A.	A key consultant in the preparations for a convention.
	Q.	What is the parliamentarian? **RONR 608**
59-8	A.	The time when the convention parliamentarian should become involved.
	Q.	What is well in advance? **RONR 608**
59-9	A.	The place for the parliamentarian during the convention meetings.
	Q.	What is seated next to the presiding officer? **RONR 608-09**
59-10	A.	The time when the most important work of convention parliamentarian is accomplished.
	Q.	What is before the convention opens? **RONR 609**
59-11	A.	These are the people who receive advice from the convention parliamentarian in arranging for that convention.
	Q.	What are president, other officers, committee chairmen? **RONR 609**

59-12 A.	Groups who should consult the parliamentarian prior to the convention.	
Q.	Who are: the chairman of every convention committee?	**RONR 609**
59-13 A.	The first business for a group of delegates.	
Q.	What is form itself into a single voting body?	**RONR 609**
59-14 A.	Relation of preliminary ceremonies to the convention business meetings.	
Q.	What is not regarded as business?	**RONR 609**
59-15 A.	When organized in accordance with the bylaws or other governing rules.	
Q.	What is acts as and in the name of the whole society.	**RONR 609**
59-16 A.	The three committee reports required to be considered and adopted for the establishment of an official convention.	
Q.	What is credentials committee, committee on standing rules, and program committee reports?	**RONR 609-10**
59-17 A.	The order of consideration of the three key committees' reports.	
Q.	What is first, credentials committee; then committee on standing rules; and finally, the program committee?	**RONR 609-10**
59-18 A.	How the committee report presenter ends his presentation.	
Q.	What is stating "by direction of the committee" unless he is not a member of the convention, in which case anyone who is a member can move the adoption of the report?	**RONR 610**
59-19 A.	The requirement for a second to a motion for adoption of committee reports.	
Q.	What is none required?	**RONR 610**
59-20 A.	The option of the chair if the presenter does not propose a motion for adoption.	
Q.	What is can call for a motion or assume the motion by stating "the question is on the adoption of the report of the ___"?	**RONR 610**
59-21 A.	Majority, two-thirds, and majority.	
Q.	What is vote required on the three reports?	**RONR 610**
59-22 A.	The point at which convention is officially organized for conducting business.	
Q.	What is upon adoption of the three separate reports: credentials, standing rules, and program?	**RONR 610**
59-23 A.	Provides the credentials forms to the constituent body.	
Q.	What is the credentials committee?	**RONR 611**

59-24 A.	Examines returned credential forms.	
Q.	What is the credentials committee?	**RONR 611**

59-25 A.	Compiles list of members entitled to register at a convention.	
Q.	What is the credentials committee?	**RONR 611-12**

59-26 A.	Performs the registration of delegates and voting members at the convention.	
Q.	What is the credentials committee?	**RONR 612**

59-27 A.	The time when the credentials committee's first report is presented to the convention.	
Q.	What is as the first item of official business?	**RONR 612**

59-28 A.	The credential committee submits supplementary reports.	
Q.	What is at the beginning of the first business meeting each day?	
Q.	What is at other times when required due to changes in registration rolls?	**RONR 612**

59-29 A.	The times the credentials committee should provide for registration.	
Q.	What is a day or two in advance of the convention and before and during each business meeting?	**RONR 613**

59-30 A.	A frequent method to assist in handling a large number of delegates.	
Q.	What is divide the membership up into sections and have a registration desk for each?	**RONR 613-14**

59-31 A.	The action taken when there is a contest between two delegates or groups of delegates and there is serious doubt as to which is entitled to be seated.	
Q.	What is both omitted from list and report the fact to the convention?	**RONR 614**

59–32 A.	Motions which are in order at a convention before the credentials report is presented.	
Q.	What are only motions relating to the consideration of the credentials report, the conduct of the meeting, or which can be made in the absence of a quorum?	**RONR 615**

59-33 A.	The total number of convention members entitled to vote.	
Q.	What is should always be included in the credentials report?	**RONR 615**

59-34 A.	"On behalf of the committee, I move that the roll of delegates hereby submitted be the official roll of voting members of the convention."	
Q.	What is how the credentials committee chairman concludes the report?	**RONR 616**

59-35 A.	A question the chair asks prior to taking the vote on the credentials report.	
Q.	What is "Are there any questions on the report?"	**RONR 616**

59-36 A.	Action which can be taken on the credentials report.	
Q.	What is debate, amend, and adopt?	**RONR 616**

59-37 A.	The method used to resolve contests between delegates.	
Q.	What is amend the report to include one contested delegate's name to the list?	**RONR 616**

59-38 A.	Limit on the scope of any single amendment to the credentials report.	
Q.	What is a single delegate or a delegation, all of whom are challenged on the same grounds?	**RONR 616**

59-39 A.	Those who can debate, amend, or vote on the credentials report.	
Q.	What are only those whose names are on the list of voting members reported by the committee?	**RONR 616**

59-40 A.	The time when a member registering late assumes full status.	
Q.	What is immediately upon being registered?	**RONR 617**

59-41 A.	Vote required when an updated report is offered with no changes.	
Q.	What is no vote?	**RONR 617**

59-42 A.	Vote required to adopt a credentials report or a supplemental credentials report.	
Q.	What is a majority vote?	**RONR 617**

59-43 A.	Responsible for being able to state the exact number of voting delegates as any time.	
Q.	What is the credentials committee?	**RONR 617**

59-44 A.	Quorum of a convention, if not prescribed in the bylaws.	
Q.	What is a majority of the number of voting members who have actually registered?	**RONR 617**

59-45 A.	When adopted, the time that the standing rules of the convention are in effect.	
Q.	What is that one convention only?	**RONR 618**

59-46 A.	Document with which the convention standing rules may not conflict.	
Q.	What is organization's bylaws?	**RONR 618**

| 59-47 | A. | The relationship of convention standing rules to parliamentary authority prescribed in bylaws. |
| | Q. | What is standing rules can modify the rules in the parliamentary authority? **RONR 618** |

| 59-48 | A. | Contains both parliamentary and non-parliamentary rules. |
| | Q. | What are convention standing rules? **RONR 618** |

| 59-49 | A. | The time when the effect of convention standing rules expires. |
| | Q. | What is at the end of the convention? **RONR 618** |

| 59-50 | A. | Frequent status of the convention standing rules from one convention to the next. |
| | Q. | What is with little change? **RONR 618** |

| 59-51 | A. | A person who should be consulted in the development of convention standing rules. |
| | Q. | What is the convention parliamentarian? **RONR 618** |

| 59-52 | A. | Rules which apply until the rules committee report is adopted. |
| | Q. | What is the rules of the organization's parliamentary authority? **RONR 618** |

| 59-53 | A. | The point where the convention standing rules are considered by the voting members. |
| | Q. | What is immediately after adoption of credentials report? **RONR 619** |

| 59-54 | A. | When every delegate has been provided with a copy of the convention standing rules and the rules do not change from year to year, or a firmly established custom of the organization applies. |
| | Q. | What is when the standing rules do not need to be read? **RONR 619** |

| 59-55 | A. | The number of votes usually taken to adopt convention standing rules. |
| | Q. | What is one vote (on the complete body of rules)? **RONR 619** |

| 59-56 | A. | The applicability of seriatim consideration to convention standing rules. |
| | Q. | What is not applicable because the rules are a group of separate main motions being offered under one enacting motion? **RONR 619** |

| 59-57 | A. | The requirement to separate out a single rule from the complete body of standing rules. |
| | Q. | What is on the demand of one member? **RONR 619** |

59-58	A.	A voting procedure for voting on a body of standing rules and any rule separated out or proposed during consideration.
	Q.	What is body of standing rules is voted on first, followed by any rules separated out or proposed for addition? **RONR 619**
59-59	A.	The vote required on the complete body of standing rules for a convention.
	Q.	What is two-thirds? **RONR 619**
59-60	A.	The vote required for a separated rule or a proposed additional rule.
	Q.	What is depends on nature of the rule? **RONR 619-20**
59-61	A.	The vote to adopt a convention standing rule proposing limits on speeches when voted on separately.
	Q.	What is two-thirds? **RONR 620**
59-62	A.	The vote for a convention standing rule concerning wearing of badges when voted on separately.
	Q.	What is majority? **RONR 620**
59-63	A.	The vote for amending an adopted convention standing rule which was not adopted individually by a majority vote.
	Q.	What is two-thirds or majority of all delegates? **RONR 620**
59-64	A.	The vote for amending a convention standing rule which was individually adopted by a majority vote.
	Q.	What is a majority vote after notice on at least the preceding day? **RONR 620**
59-65	A.	Vote required to suspend a convention standing rule (except one prescribing the parliamentary authority) for a specific purpose.
	Q.	What is majority? **RONR 620-21**
59-66	A.	The rules that are in force when a convention standing rule is suspended.
	Q.	What is rules contained in the parliamentary authority specified by bylaws (or by a rule of the convention)? **RONR 621**
59-67	A.	The duration for which a convention standing rule cannot be suspended.
	Q.	What is the remainder of the session? **RONR 621**
59-68	A.	Suspension of a standing rule with a single application.
	Q.	What is not allowed? **RONR 621**
59-69	A.	The result of adoption of the program committee's report.
	Q.	What is becomes convention's order of business? **RONR 624**

| 59-70 | A. | Series of addresses, forums, workshops, exhibits, tours, and other activities. |
| | Q. | What is commonly part of the convention program? **RONR 624** |

59-71	A.	Items which the program committee needs to be authorized to arrange.
	Q.	What is engage outside speakers or entertainment?
	Q.	What is work out an order of business allotting appropriate amounts of time to each subject?
	Q.	What is all necessary advance arrangements? **RONR 625**

| 59-72 | A. | The reasons a convention's order of business must be more detailed than for a normal meeting. |
| | Q. | What are adherence to a prearranged schedule is imperative and each member has a right to know when business is scheduled? **RONR 625-26** |

| 59-73 | A. | When the program is split into two parts, the name for the detailed business portion. |
| | Q. | What is the agenda? **RONR 626** |

| 59-74 | A. | Information which should be made available to delegates before their arrival at the convention site. |
| | Q. | What is times of registration and pre-convention events? **RONR 626** |

| 59-75 | A. | The proper order of events for the opening ceremonies of a convention. |
| | Q. | What is invocation, followed by national anthem, followed by pledge of allegiance to the flag? **RONR 626** |

| 59-76 | A. | Follows an address of welcome by a local public official. |
| | Q. | What is remarks of acknowledgment and appreciation? **RONR 626-27** |

| 59-77 | A. | Information that should be included in the business meeting program or agenda. |
| | Q. | What is specific times for opening and closing meetings and the specific order in which the subjects or classes of subjects are to come up? **RONR 627** |

| 59-78 | A. | The treatment of an important policy question set for a particular hour in the agenda. |
| | Q. | What is as if it were a special order? **RONR 627** |

| 59-79 | A. | The order of the presentation of officers' reports. |
| | Q. | What is in the order the offices are listed in the bylaws? **RONR 627** |

59-80	A.	Place in the order of business for consideration and adoption of the report of the auditors.
	Q.	What is immediately following the treasurer's report? **RONR 627**
59-81	A.	The point in the agenda when the report of the board is presented.
	Q.	What is following reports of officers? **RONR 627**
59-82	A.	The time when a committee report containing a resolution or motion is presented.
	Q.	What is usually before the report of the resolutions committee? **RONR 628**
59-83	A.	The time when announcements are made at a convention.
	Q.	What is immediately preceding the adjournment of each meeting? **RONR 628**
59-84	A.	Methods for handling the approval of minutes of the convention.
	Q.	What is first order of business each day (after the first day) of convention?
	Q.	What is authority is given to the board or a special committee to approve the minutes of the last day? **RONR 628**
59-85	A.	The method for handling business unfinished at the end of a day of a convention.
	Q.	What is taken up immediately (following approval of the minutes) at the next meeting unless there is a conflict with a special order? **RONR 628**
59-86	A.	The recommended placement for the election of officers on the agenda.
	Q.	What is relatively early? **RONR 629**
59-87	A.	The usual time when installation ceremonies are held.
	Q.	What is at the closing banquet? **RONR 629**
59-88	A.	The effect of the program or agenda even before it has been adopted.
	Q.	What is serves as guide to the chair? **RONR 629**
59-89	A.	The point in the program when the program committee makes its report.
	Q.	What is immediately after adoption of the convention standing rules? **RONR 629**
59-90	A.	The vote required for the adoption of the program of a convention.
	Q.	What is majority? **RONR 630**

59-91	A.	The vote required to change the program once it has been adopted.
	Q.	What is two-thirds, or majority of all the delegates or other "voting members" of the convention who have been registered, or unanimous consent? ***RONR 630***
59-92	A.	Persons who should be included on the convention arrangements committee.
	Q.	What are individuals who have had experience at prior conventions? ***RONR 631***
59-93	A.	Committees that the convention arrangements committee must work with closely.
	Q.	What are the credentials committee and the program committee? ***RONR 631***
59-94	A.	Duty often assigned to the program committee concerning guest speakers.
	Q.	What is meeting them at the airport or other point of arrival? ***RONR 632-33***
59-95	A.	Responsible for providing directions to the convention site and advance program to the delegates.
	Q.	What is the convention arrangements committee? ***RONR 632***
59-96	A.	Consideration in setting up the seating arrangement.
	Q.	What is separate seating for delegates? ***RONR 632***
59-97	A.	Responsible for providing pages, messengers, ushers, and other door-keepers.
	Q.	What is the convention arrangements committee? ***RONR 632***
59-98	A.	Two other names often used for the resolutions committee.
	Q.	What are reference committee and platform committee? ***RONR 633***
59-99	A.	The general function of the resolutions committee.
	Q.	What is screening of all original main motions that have not been screened by another committee? ***RONR 633***
59-100	A.	Justification for the limitation imposed on the rights of members to introduce main motions by use of a resolutions committee.
	Q.	What is the need to keep within a schedule?
	Q.	What is the need to dispose of a large amount of business within a short time? ***RONR 633***
59-101	A.	The simplest situation for processing a main motion when there is a resolutions committee.
	Q.	What is member makes motion and the chair immediately refers it to the resolutions committee? ***RONR 633-34***

59-102A.	A requirement in some organizations, established by bylaw provision or a permanent rule, for when resolutions must be proposed.
Q.	What is must be submitted prior to the convention for review by the committee in advance? **RONR 634**

59-103A.	The usual source for introduction of main motions at a convention.
Q.	What is only the delegate (members of the convention)? **RONR 634**

59-104A.	Only way that a non-delegate can speak or make a motion at a convention.
Q.	What is only with the consent of the convention? **RONR 634**

59-105A.	The usual power of a resolutions committee.
Q.	What is only to put resolutions into proper form, eliminate duplications, and arrange in logical sequence? **RONR 635**

59-106A.	Make substantive alterations to resolutions.
Q.	What is authority sometimes given to resolutions committee? **RONR 635**

59-107A.	The customary rule with regard to the requirement of the resolutions committee to report all resolutions referred to it.
Q.	What is must report all resolutions and, if it wishes, report a resolution with "no recommendation"? **RONR 635**

59-108A.	Power sometimes given to the resolutions committee which usually requires a high vote (three-fourths or two-thirds) within the committee.
Q.	What is "not to report" or to withhold a resolution? **RONR 635-36**

59-109A.	A power the convention, by majority vote, should have concerning withheld resolutions.
Q.	What is require the resolutions committee to report a resolution? **RONR 636**

59-110A.	Preamble words used when the resolution is a platform or policy statement.
Q.	What is "Believing ..."? **RONR 636**

59-111A.	Setting forth its views, aims, and aspirations.
Q.	What is nature of a platform resolution? **RONR 636**

59-112A.	Enacting words used when the resolution is a platform or policy statement.
Q.	What are "Affirm," "Assures," "Condemns," "Calls upon," and the like? **RONR 636**

59-113A.	This group who usually prepares the courtesy resolution or resolutions.	
Q.	What is the resolutions committee?	**RONR 637**

59-114A.	Used to express appreciation to those who arranged accommodations or rendered service.	
Q.	What is a courtesy resolution?	**RONR 637**

59-115A.	The involvement of the sponsor of a resolution with the resolutions committee.	
Q.	What is allowed to explain resolution to the committee?	**RONR 637-38**

59-116A.	The name applied to the time period(s) when the resolutions committee invites information and comment on resolutions.	
Q.	What is open "hearing(s)"?	**RONR 638**

59-117A.	The resolutions committee conducts its voting under this condition.	
Q.	What is in executive session?	**RONR 638**

59-118A.	Action that is considered complete on a motion reported out from the resolutions committee.	
Q.	What is that it has been properly moved and seconded?	**RONR 638**

59-119A.	Special rules of debate sometimes used for resolutions of major significance at a convention.	
Q.	What is limit total time for debate and divide the time between the opposing sides?	**RONR 639**

Here is the Answer! What is the Question? Book 5

189

Section 60 - Conventions Not of a Permanent Society

Robert's Rules of Order Newly Revised, 11th Edition - Pages 640-42

60-1	A.	Conventions not involving a permanent organization that are called for a specific purpose are similar to a mass meeting in this regard.
	Q.	What is have no bylaws or officers when called? **RONR 640**
60-2	A.	For a convention not of a permanent society, group appointed to secure the hall and accommodations for the delegates.
	Q.	What is convention arrangements committee? **RONR 640**
60-3	A.	For a convention not of a permanent society, group appointed to make preliminary arrangements for the convention.
	Q.	What is convention arrangements committee? **RONR 640**
60-4	A.	For a convention not of a permanent society, group appointed to perform the other coordinating and arranging duties assigned to it.
	Q.	What is convention arrangements committee? **RONR 640**
60-5	A.	The first action to be taken at a convention not of a permanent society.
	Q.	What is elect a temporary chairman? **RONR 640**
60-6	A.	Action following the election of the chairman for a convention not of a permanent society.
	Q.	What is elect a temporary secretary? **RONR 640**
60-7	A.	Action following the election of a secretary for a convention not of a permanent society.
	Q.	What is appointment (or ratification of prior selection) of the credentials, rules, and program committees? **RONR 640**
60-8	A.	Action while awaiting the report of the credentials committee.
	Q.	What is listen to talks? **RONR 641**
60-9	A.	The principal purpose in electing a temporary chairman first and a permanent chairman later.
	Q.	What is to enable the temporary chairman to preside over the convention while it acts upon any matters relating to contested seats? **RONR 641**
60-10	A.	The reason for waiting to elect permanent chairman until after adoption of credentials report.
	Q.	What is to be elected by delegates on the permanent roll of the convention? **RONR 641**

60-11	A.	If a convention has been called to form a permanent society, this action is appropriate after adoption of the three standard committee reports.
	Q.	What is to adopt a resolution expressing the intention to form a permanent society? **RONR 641**
60-12	A.	Action that must be taken at the convention before the permanent society is formed.
	Q.	What is bylaws must be adopted? **RONR 641-42**
60-13	A.	The procedure for selecting the nominating committee which should be followed at a convention intending to form a permanent society.
	Q.	What is the process prescribed by the bylaws as closely as possible? **RONR 642**
60-14	A.	The time when officers elected for new society assume office.
	Q.	What is immediately after election? **RONR 642**

CHAPTER XX: DISCIPLINARY PROCEDURES

Section 61 – Disciplinary Procedures

Robert's Rules of Order Newly Revised, 11th Edition - Pages 643-50

61-1	A.	General requirement understood for members of most societies.
	Q.	What is be of honorable character and reputation? **RONR 643**
61-2	A.	The ultimate right of any organization.
	Q.	What is to make and enforce its own rules?
	Q.	What is require that its members refrain from conduct injurious to the organization or its purposes? **RONR 643**
61-3	A.	Reason to not be allowed to remain a member.
	Q.	What is if retention will do harm to the organization? **RONR 643**
61-4	A.	Censure, fine, suspension, or expulsion.
	Q.	What is generally available punishments of a member? **RONR 643**
61-5	A.	The extreme penalty that an organization or society can impose.
	Q.	What is expulsion? **RONR 643**
61-6	A.	Where an organization may specify a number of offenses outside meeting.
	Q.	What is in the bylaws? **RONR 643-44**
61-7	A.	"Tending to injure the good name of the organization, disturb its well-being, or hamper it in its work."
	Q.	What is types of conduct which is subject to punishment? **RONR 644**
61-8	A.	Of prime importance in the handling of a case requiring disciplinary action.
	Q.	What is proper and tactful handling? **RONR 644**
61-9	A.	Suggested first action in attempting to resolve a disciplinary situation.
	Q.	What is obtain a satisfactory solution of the matter quietly and informally? **RONR 644**
61-10	A.	The two cases of conduct subject to disciplinary action.
	Q.	What are offenses occurring in a meeting and offenses by members outside a meeting? **RONR 644**
61-11	A.	The rights of a society concerning meetings.
	Q.	What are to determine who may be present and to control its hall? **RONR 644**

| 61-12 A. | The rights of all members concerning meetings. |
| Q. | What is to attend [with two exceptions]? **RONR 644** |

| 61-13 A. | The exceptions to the member's right to attend meetings of the society. |
| Q. | What are where bylaws provide for suspension of members who fall in arrears in payment of dues or when the society, by vote and as a penalty, has forbidden attendance for a specific offense? **RONR 644** |

| 61-14 A. | Rights of a society concerning nonmembers at a meeting. |
| Q. | What is right to exclude? **RONR 644** |

| 61-15 A. | The way disorderly nonmembers can be excluded from a meeting. |
| Q. | What is by ruling of the chair? **RONR 644** |

61-16 A.	Action which will exclude nonmembers from all or a portion of the meeting.
Q.	What is adoption of a rule on the subject?
Q.	What is a motion to "go into executive session"? **RONR 644-45**

| 61-17 A. | The type of motion that excludes all but essential nonmembers from a meeting. |
| Q. | What is a question of privilege? **RONR 644-45** |

| 61-18 A. | The obligation that applies to everyone present at a meeting. |
| Q. | What is to obey the legitimate orders of the presiding officer? **RONR 645** |

61-19 A.	In a disorderly situation, action the chair should not do under any circumstances.
Q.	What is attempt to drown out a disorderly member?
Q.	What is permit himself to be drawn into a verbal duel? **RONR 645**

| 61-20 A. | Appropriate action by chair for slight breaches of order. |
| Q. | What is raps lightly with the gavel, points out the fault, and advises the member to avoid it? **RONR 645** |

| 61-21 A. | Least severe formal procedure for breaches of order in a meeting. |
| Q. | What is calling a member to order? **RONR 645-46** |

61-22 A.	Grounds for a member to be called to order.
Q.	What is repeatedly questions the motives of other members whom he mentions by name?
Q.	What is persists in speaking on completely irrelevant matters in debate? **RONR 645-46**

| 61-23 A. | During a meeting, persons who can call a member to order. |
| Q. | What is the chair or any other member? **RONR 646** |

61-24	A.	The motion used by another member to call a member to order.
	Q.	What is a point of order? **RONR 646**
61-25	A.	Action the chair directs a member to take when he has been called to order.
	Q.	What is be seated? **RONR 646**
61-26	A.	The action taken by the chair after the member who has been called to order is seated.
	Q.	What is states the breach involved and puts the question on allowing the member to continue to speak? **RONR 646**
61-27	A.	The question, which is undebatable, the chair puts to the assembly following the calling of a member to order.
	Q.	What is "Shall the member be allowed to continue speaking?" **RONR 646**
61-28	A.	The action that the chair can take in cases of obstinate or grave breach of order by a member.
	Q.	What is "naming" an offender? **RONR 646**
61-29	A.	What "naming" an offender amounts to.
	Q.	What is preferring charges? **RONR 646**
61-30	A.	The first step taken by the chair when proceeding to "naming" an offender.
	Q.	What is direct the secretary to take down objectionable or disorderly words used by the member? **RONR 646**
61-31	A.	What happens to the secretary's recording of objectionable or disorderly words used by a member.
	Q.	What is entered into the minutes if the member is "named"? **RONR 646**
61-32	A.	The group that has the power to impose a penalty or to order the offending member removed from the hall.
	Q.	What is the assembly? **RONR 646**
61-33	A.	An action that is not needed for offenses which occur during a meeting.
	Q.	What is a formal trial with witnesses? **RONR 646**
61-34	A.	The form of the declaration made by the chair in naming a member.
	Q.	What is addressed to the offender by name and in the second person? **RONR 646-47**

61-35	A.	The group that has the choice of dropping the matter when a member "named" obeys the chair's directive.
	Q.	What is the assembly? **RONR 647**
61-36	A.	Two actions of a member, who has been "named," that can resolve the case.
	Q.	What are by an apology or a withdrawal of objectionable statements or remarks? **RONR 647**
61-37	A.	The proposal made by a member who doesn't feel the "named" member's response is sufficient.
	Q.	What is move to order a penalty? **RONR 647**
61-38	A.	The proposal of the chair if he doesn't feel the "named" member's response is sufficient.
	Q.	What is asks "What penalty shall be imposed on the member?" **RONR 647**
61-39	A.	Penalties which can be proposed against a "named" member.
	Q.	What is directed to make an apology, censured, required to leave hall for the remainder of the meeting or until he is prepared to apologize, suspended, or expelled? **RONR 647**
61-40	A.	Vote necessary to require "named" member to leave the hall during consideration of his penalty.
	Q.	What is majority? **RONR 647**
61-41	A.	The right of "named" member before he is required to leave the hall.
	Q.	What is to present his defense briefly? **RONR 647**
61-42	A.	Require the vote on the imposition of a penalty to be taken by ballot.
	Q.	What is action that can be demanded by a single member? **RONR 647**
61-43	A.	Vote required to expel a "named" member from membership.
	Q.	What is two-thirds? **RONR 648**
61-44	A.	What the member exposes himself to if he refuses to leave the hall.
	Q.	What is more severe disciplinary action? **RONR 648**
61-45	A.	Rights of nonmembers allowed in the hall during a meeting, as guests of the organization.
	Q.	What is have no rights with reference to the proceedings? **RONR 648**
61-46	A.	The person who has the power to require a nonmember to leave the hall, or to order their removal.
	Q.	What is the chair? **RONR 648**

61-47	A.	The right to appeal the chair's order for a nonmember to leave the hall.
	Q.	What is any member, but not the nonmember so ordered? **RONR 648**
61-48	A.	Action the chair may take to enforce an order to leave the hall.
	Q.	What is appoint a committee to escort the offender to the door?
	Q.	What is ask the sergeant-at-arms to escort the offender to the door? **RONR 648**
61-49	A.	An alternative to having a committee or the sergeant-at-arms escort an offender to the door if the organization is prepared to press charges.
	Q.	What is request that he be removed by the police? **RONR 648-49**
61-50	A.	Power of an appointed escort committee or the sergeant-at-arms in escorting an offender to the door.
	Q.	What is to use the minimum force necessary? **RONR 649**
61-51	A.	Potential problem with using force to remove an offender from the hall.
	Q.	What is the person(s) who applied the force may be held liable for damages? **RONR 649**
61-52	A.	Action suggested in cases where possibly serious annoyance by hostile persons is anticipated.
	Q.	What is arrange for presence of police or guards from a security service agency? **RONR 649**
61-53	A.	When improper conduct occurs elsewhere than at a meeting, the steps that are required to process disciplinary action.
	Q.	What is charges must be preferred and a formal trial held? **RONR 649**
61-54	A,	Action required for improper conduct at a meeting if immediate action was not taken.
	Q.	What is charges must be preferred and a formal trial held? **RONR 649**

Section 62 - Removal from Office and Other Remedies for Dereliction of Duty in Office or Misconduct

Robert's Rules of Order Newly Revised, 11th Edition - Pages 650-54

62-1	A.	Available if officers neglect those duties, abuse their authority, or engage in other misconduct that calls into question their fitness for office.
	Q.	What are disciplinary procedures? **RONR 650**
62-2	A.	Form of discipline that the bylaws may permit.
	Q.	What is removal from office at pleasure of assembly? **RONR 650**
62-3	A.	Action to be taken if the chair at a meeting acts improperly.
	Q.	What is raise a point of order? **RONR 650**
62-4	A.	Action when the chair ignores a point of order motion three times.
	Q.	What is member can put the point of order to a vote? **RONR 650**
62-5	A.	Condition when a member, from floor, can put a motion to vote without debate.
	Q.	What is when the chair ignores a properly made and seconded motion? **RONR 651**
62-6	A.	When the chair can be declared vacant and a new chairman elected.
	Q.	What is if the occupant is appointed or elected chairman pro tem? **RONR 651**
62-7	A.	Classification of a motion to declare chair vacant and establish a new election.
	Q.	What is a question of privilege affecting the assembly and is an incidental main motion? **RONR 651-52**
62-8	A.	Vote required to adopt motion to declare chair vacant if occupant is chairman pro tem.
	Q.	What is a majority vote? **RONR 652**
62-9	A.	Action which may be taken if the chair refuses to state a motion to declare the chair vacant.
	Q.	What is maker can state and process the motion? **RONR 652n**
62-10	A.	The motion to be used to remove the chair's authority to preside.
	Q.	What is Suspend the Rules? **RONR 652**
62-11	A.	Reason that a chair's authority can be removed even when bylaws state the president shall preside at all meetings.
	Q.	What is provision is clearly in the nature of a rule of order? **RONR 652n**

62-12	A.	Action the president must take after stating the motion to Suspend the Rules to remove his authority to preside.
	Q.	What is turn the chair over to someone else to process the motion?
		RONR 652

62-13	A.	Action which may be taken if the president refuses to state a motion to Suspend the Rules and remove his authority to preside.
	Q.	What is the maker can state and process the motion from the floor?
		RONR 652

62-14	A.	Length of time that a motion to suspend the rules and remove presiding authority from the president is effective.
	Q.	What is for one session? **RONR 652**

62-15	A.	Action which the motion to suspend the rules to prevent the president from presiding does NOT prevent.
	Q.	What is administrative duties of the position? **RONR 653**

62-16	A.	Assembly action after adoption of a motion to suspend the rules to prevent the president to preside.
	Q.	What is the ranking vice-president has the duty to preside?**RONR 653**

62-17	A.	Method of removal from office when term is defined as X years OR until successor is elected.
	Q.	What is motion to remove the officer? **RONR 653**

62-18	A.	Vote requirement for a motion to remove an officer.
	Q.	What is a two-thirds vote (with no notice)?
	Q.	What is a majority vote with notice?
	Q.	What is a majority of the total membership? **RONR 653**

62-19	A.	Type of motion to remove an officer.
	Q.	What is a question of privilege affecting the assembly? **RONR 653-54**

62-20	A.	Method of removal from office when term is defined as X years or as X years AND until their successor is elected.
	Q.	What is only for cause and with a trial? **RONR 654**

Section 63 - Investigation and Trial

Robert's Rules of Order Newly Revised, 11th Edition - Pages 654-59

63-1	A.	Process for removal of an officer for cause or discipline of member for improper conduct.	
	Q.	What is prefer charges and formal trial?	**RONR 654**
63-2	A.	Action which may be taken to remove an officer and discipline him as well.	
	Q.	What is both charges may be combined?	**RONR 654n**
63-3	A.	Effect of expulsion from membership on holding office when bylaws make membership a required qualification.	
	Q.	What is expulsion results in removal from office?	**RONR 654n**
63-4	A.	Status of society to enforce its own standards.	
	Q.	What is a right?	**RONR 655**
63-5	A.	Society's right to support enforcement of its own standards.	
	Q.	What is to investigate the character of its members and officers?	**RONR 655**
63-6	A.	Status of any information which results from a disciplinary investigation.	
	Q.	What is should not be revealed to any person outside the society?	**RONR 655**
63-7	A.	Session status for trial and for resolutions leading up to a trial.	
	Q.	What is must be considered in executive session?	**RONR 655**
63-8	A.	Can be disclosed if a member is expelled or an officer is removed from office.	
	Q.	What is just that fact?	**RONR 655**
63-9	A.	Can be revealed in association to a disciplinary investigation and trial.	
	Q.	What is nothing other than the result of the trial?	**RONR 655**
63-10	A.	Status of the establishment of guilt in the trial.	
	Q.	What is only the society's judgment of a member's fitness for membership or office?	**RONR 655**
63-11	A.	Type of evidence allowed in a society's trial (but not in a legal trial).	
	Q.	What is hearsay evidence?	**RONR 655**
63-12	A.	Status of witnesses during the trial.	
	Q.	What is not sworn?	**RONR 655**

63-13	A.	Right of a member or officer concerning allegations against his good name.
	Q.	What is made by charges brought on reasonable grounds?
	Q.	What is due process?
	Q.	What is to be informed of charge and given time to prepare his defense?
	Q.	What is to appear and defend himself?
	Q.	What is to be fairly treated? **RONR 656**
63-14	A.	Action that a member may take if guilty of the charge.
	Q.	What is submit his resignation? **RONR 656**
63-15	A.	Action the society should take prior to charges being preferred.
	Q.	What is offer member the opportunity to resign quietly? **RONR 656**
63-16	A.	Obligation of the society to suggest or accept resignation.
	Q.	What is none? **RONR 656**
63-17	A.	Absent any specific steps detailed in the bylaws, steps for a trial.
	Q.	What is (1) confidential investigation, (2) preferral of charges, (3) formal notification of accused, (4) trial, and (5) assembly's review of findings? **RONR 656**
63-18	A.	Qualification of members of the investigation committee.
	Q.	What is known integrity and good judgment? **RONR 656-57**
63-19	A.	Task of the investigation committee.
	Q.	What is investigate to determine whether to recommend further action? **RONR 656-57**
63-20	A.	Action which initiates an investigation and trial.
	Q.	What is adoption of a motion that establishes an investigating committee? **RONR 657**
63-21	A.	Action if investigation committee finds allegations are well-founded.
	Q.	What is report resolutions covering its recommendations? **RONR 657**
63-22	A.	Details of allegation to be included in first resolution.
	Q.	What is as little as possible? **RONR 657**
63-23	A.	An individual member, even with proof, cannot do this.
	Q.	What is prefer charges? **RONR 657**
63-24	A.	Status of a resolution preferring charges presented by a member.
	Q.	What is out of order? **RONR 657**

| 63-25 | A. | First resolution which implies the truth of specific rumors or contains insinuations unfavorable to an officer or member. |
| | Q. | What is an improper resolution? **RONR 658** |

| 63-26 | A. | Power of the investigating committee to require anyone to appear before it. |
| | Q. | What is none? **RONR 658** |

| 63-27 | A. | Duty of the investigating committee. |
| | Q. | What is make an effort to learn all the relevant facts? **RONR 658** |

| 63-28 | A. | May be used to form an opinion but cannot be reported to the society. |
| | Q. | What is information obtained in strict confidence? **RONR 658** |

63-29	A.	Specific action by investigating committee required by fairness.
	Q.	What is reasonable attempt to meet with the accused?
	Q.	What is reasonable attempt to get the accused's side of the story? **RONR 658**

| 63-30 | A. | Something the investigation committee might suggest to the accused. |
| | Q. | What is to rectify the situation or to resign? **RONR 658** |

63-31	A.	When the investigation committee finds no need for a trial.
	Q.	What is committee's opinion is favorable to the accused?
	Q.	What is committee finds matter can be resolved satisfactorily? **RONR 658**

| 63-32 | A. | What assembly can still do even if the committee report recommends no trial. |
| | Q. | What is can still prefer charges? **RONR 658n** |

| 63-33 | A. | Recommendations when investigating committee finds substance to the allegations. |
| | Q. | What is a resolution preferring charges, arranging for a trial, and, if desired, suspending the rights of the accused? **RONR 659** |

| 63-34 | A. | Reasonable time to allow accused to prepare his defense. |
| | Q. | What is thirty days? **RONR 660** |

| 63-35 | A. | Policy for holding meeting for the trial. |
| | Q. | What is meeting is devoted exclusively to the matter? **RONR 660** |

| 63-36 | A. | Process if there is to be a regular meeting before the date for the trial. |
| | Q. | What is establish the trial as a special meeting? **RONR 660-61** |

63-37	A.	Special meeting when bylaws do not provide for special meetings.
	Q.	What is allowed for a trial? **RONR 661n**
63-38	A.	Alternative to assembly meeting for delicate trial.
	Q.	What is establish a committee to conduct the trial? **RONR 661**
63-39	A.	What a charge does.
	Q.	What is sets forth an offense? **RONR 662**
63-40	A.	What a specification does.
	Q.	What is states what is alleged to have been done? **RONR 662**
63-41	A.	Role of specification(s) relative to the charge.
	Q.	What is constitutes an instance of the offense? **RONR 662**
63-42	A.	"Conduct tending to injure the good name of the organization, disturb its well- being, or hamper it in its work."
	Q.	What is a charge against a member? **RONR 662**
63-43	A.	"Misconduct in office," "neglect of duty in office," or "conduct that renders him unfit for office."
	Q.	What is charges against an officer? **RONR 662**
63-44	A.	Requirement for each separate charge in the resolution.
	Q.	What is at least one specification? **RONR 662**
63-45	A.	To make each specification no broader than is believed sufficient to establish the validity of the charge.
	Q.	What is specification is carefully worded? **RONR 662**
63-46	A.	Exception to suspension of all membership rights of the accused.
	Q.	What is rights that relate to the trial? **RONR 662**
63-47	A.	Persons with the task of presenting the evidence against the accused.
	Q.	What are the managers? **RONR 662**
63-48	A.	Relationship of the managers to the society.
	Q.	What is must be members? **RONR 662**
63-49	A.	Tasks of the managers.
	Q.	What is NOT to act as prosecutors?
	Q.	What is to strive that the trial will get at the truth?
	Q.	What is that the outcome will be just? **RONR 662-63**
63-50	A.	Secretary's action following adopting of resolutions ordering a trial.
	Q.	What is sends information about trial to accused by method which confirms delivery? **RONR 663**

63-51	A.	What secretary should have at hand at the trial.	
	Q.	What is proof of the delivery to accused's address?	**RONR 663**
63-52	A.	Definition of a trial.	
	Q.	What is a formal hearing on the validity of the charges?	**RONR 663**
63-53	A.	Who presents the evidence against the accused officer or member at the trial.	
	Q.	What is the managers?	**RONR 663-64**
63-54	A.	Rights of the accused at the trial.	
	Q.	What is represented by counsel?	
	Q.	What is right to speak and produce witnesses?	**RONR 664**
63-55	A.	Action when charges are found to be true.	
	Q.	What is a penalty may be imposed or recommended?	**RONR 664**
63-56	A.	Action if charges are not substantiated.	
	Q.	What is all rights previously suspended are automatically restored?	**RONR 664**
63-57	A.	Status of defense counsel unless permitted by the assembly or trial committee.	
	Q.	What is must be members of the society?	**RONR 664**
63-58	A.	When nonmember witnesses can be in the trial room.	
	Q.	What is only when testifying?	**RONR 664**
63-59	A.	Action if the accused fails to appear at time of trial.	
	Q.	What is trial proceeds without him?	**RONR 664**
63-60	A.	Adopt a resolution to govern the trial by specifying details of the procedure.	
	Q.	What is what the assembly can do?	**RONR 664**
63-61	A.	Vote required to adopt a resolution specifying details consistent with those contained in RONR.	
	Q.	What is majority?	**RONR 664**
63-62	A.	Vote required to modify the procedure contained in RONR.	
	Q.	What is previous notice and two-thirds?	
	Q.	What is majority of the entire membership?	**RONR 664n**
63-63	A.	Requirement if time limits are imposed on parts of the trial.	
	Q.	What is allow defense at least equal time?	**RONR 664**
63-64	A.	Required in order to suspend any time limits established for the trial.	
	Q.	What is consent of the defense?	**RONR 664**

63-65 A.	Action the chair should take in calling the trial meeting to order.	
Q.	What is call attention to the fact that the meeting is in executive session and to the attendant obligation of secrecy?	**RONR 664-65**
63-66 A.	First action in the proceeding of the trial.	
Q.	What is secretary reads the charge and specifications?	**RONR 665**
63-67 A.	Action following reading of the charge and specifications.	
Q.	What is accused pleads guilty or not guilty to each specification in order and then to the charge?	**RONR 665**
63-68 A.	Action if the accused pleads guilty to the charge, after brief statement of facts..	
Q.	What is proceed directly to determination of penalty?	**RONR 665**
63-69 A.	Opening statements by both sides, managers first.	
Q.	What is first step in actual trial procedure?	**RONR 665**
63-70 A.	Second step in actual trial procedure.	
Q.	What is testimony of witnesses produced by the managers?	**RONR 665**
63-71 A.	Third step in actual trial procedure.	
Q.	What is testimony of defense witnesses?	**RONR 665**
63-72 A.	Fourth step in actual trial procedure.	
Q.	What is rebuttal witnesses on behalf of society and then on behalf of the defense?	**RONR 665**
63-73 A.	Closing arguments by both sides at the trial.	
Q.	What is the last step of the actual trial?	**RONR 665**
63-74 A.	Entitled to the floor during the actual trial process.	
Q.	What is only managers and the defense?	**RONR 665**
63-75 A.	Person to whom the managers and defense address.	
Q.	What is the chair?	**RONR 665**
63-76 A.	Cross-examination, re-direct-examination, and re-cross-examination of a witness.	
Q.	What is permitted during trial?	**RONR 665**
63-77 A.	Action which can be taken relative to the chair's direction or rulings during the trial.	
Q.	What is any member can appeal?	**RONR 666**
63-78 A.	Debate status of an appeal made during the trial.	
Q.	What is undebatable?	**RONR 666**

63-79	A.	Action chair may take before providing direction or a ruling during the trial.
	Q.	What is submit to assembly for an undebatable vote? **_RONR 666_**

63-80	A.	Persons who may propose modifications to the resolution governing of the trial.
	Q.	What is the managers or the defense or the chair? **_RONR 666_**

63-81	A.	Rules for processing a proposed modification to the resolution governing the trial.
	Q.	What is undebatable; same vote as required for the motion to amend something previously adopted? **_RONR 666_**

63-82	A.	Action if a member of the assembly has a question for a witness, manager or defense.
	Q.	What is question is delivered in writing to the presiding officer? **_RONR 666_**

63-83	A.	Motions which are in order during the trial.
	Q.	What is the five privileged motions?
	Q.	What is those that relate to the conduct of the meeting or the trial? **_RONR 666_**

63-84	A.	Process for a member to make a motion during the trial.
	Q.	What is delivered to presiding officer in writing? **_RONR 666_**

63-85	A.	Action required of the accused following closing arguments.
	Q.	What is must leave the room? **_RONR 667_**

63-86	A.	Question on the finding as to the guilt of the accused.
	Q.	What is stated by chair following closing arguments? **_RONR 667_**

63-87	A.	Handling of the charges and specifications.
	Q.	What is each specification / charge is read, opened to debate, and voted on separately? **_RONR 667_**

63-88	A.	Status of a charge when accused is found not guilty of associated specifications.
	Q.	What is automatically found not guilty of charge? **_RONR 667_**

63-89	A.	Action that can be taken when accused is found guilty on a specification but not on the associated charge.
	Q.	What is may be found guilty on a lesser charge? **_RONR 667_**

63-90	A.	Process by which a penalty is determined.
	Q.	What is manager (or member) offers an appropriate motion? **_RONR 667-68_**

63-91 A.	Status of the motion specifying a penalty.	
Q.	What is debatable and amendable?	**RONR 668**

63-92 A.	Require ballot vote on question of guilt or the question of the penalty.	
Q.	What is on demand of a single member?	**RONR 668**

63-93 A.	Censure or removal from office.	
Q.	What is usual penalties for an officer?	**RONR 668**

63-94 A.	Vote required to adopt the motion prescribing the penalty.	
Q.	What is majority?	**RONR 668**

63-95 A.	Censure, fine, suspension, or expulsion.	
Q.	What is usual penalties for a member?	**RONR 668**

63-96 A.	Vote required for expulsion.	
Q.	What is two-thirds?	**RONR 668**

63-97 A.	Morally convinced that the accused is guilty.	
Q.	What is member who votes for a finding of guilty?	**RONR 668**

63-98 A.	Requirement when trial is held by a committee.	
Q.	What is committee reports to assembly?	**RONR 668**

63-99 A.	Status of the meeting when the trial committee reports.	
Q.	What is in executive session?	**RONR 668**

63-100 A.	Content of trial committee report when committee finding is guilty.	
Q.	What is resolution covering recommended penalty?	**RONR 668**

63-101 A.	Right of the accused after committee report is presented to assembly.	
Q.	What is to make a statement of the case?	**RONR 668**

63-102 A.	Committee action when accused makes a statement following submission of the committee report.	
Q.	What is has opportunity to present a statement in rebuttal?	**RONR 668**

63-103 A.	Action the accused, and defense counsel if not members, must take following submission of the trial committee's report and associated statements, if any.	
Q.	What is leave the room?	**RONR 668**

63-104 A.	Action the assembly can take on the trial committee's recommendations of a penalty.	
Q.	What is accept the recommendation, decline to impose any penalty, or reduce the recommended penalty?	**RONR 669**

63-105A.	Action the assembly CANNOT take on the trial committee's recommendation of a penalty.
Q.	What is increase the penalty? **RONR 669**
63-106A.	When the assembly CANNOT impose any penalty.
Q.	What is trial committee has found the accused not guilty? **RONR 669**
63-107A.	Sometimes provided in bylaws to simplify the handling of disciplinary issues.
Q.	What is a committee on discipline? **RONR 669**
63-108A.	Normally prescribed duties of a committee on discipline.
Q.	What is be alert to disciplinary problems?
Q.	What is investigate disciplinary problems?
Q.	What is introduce necessary resolutions?
Q.	What is manage the case in the event of a trial? **RONR 669**
63-109A.	Additional duty sometimes assigned to the committee on discipline.
Q.	What is hearing the actual trial? **RONR 669**
63-110A.	Process when committee on discipline has duty to hear the trial.
Q.	What is use different subcommittees to investigate and to conduct the trial? **RONR 669**
63-111A.	Power usually NOT given to the committee on discipline.
Q.	What is power to impose a penalty? **RONR 669**
63-112A.	Group that usually imposes the penalty when there is a committee of discipline.
Q.	What is the assembly? **RONR 669**
63-113A.	Advantages to having a committee on discipline.
Q.	What is avoids unduly inconveniencing the society?
Q.	What is promotes the avoidance of scandal?
Q.	What is promotes settlement of disciplinary problems without an actual trial? **RONR 669**

www.ingramcontent.com/pod-product-compliance
Lightning Source LLC
Chambersburg PA
CBHW080237270326

41926CB00020B/4281